#SheWins 2

Stories and Photographs of Women
Who Survived Domestic Abuse

Alisa Divine

Personal Power Press, Inc.
Bay City, Michigan

#SheWins
Alisa Divine

#SheWins 2

**Stories and Photographs of Women
Who Survived Domestic Abuse**

©2021 Alisa Divine and Personal Power Press

Library of Congress Control Number: 2021914974
ISBN: 978-0-9821568-1-0

Printed in the United States of America
Personal Power Press, Inc.
Bay City, MI 48706

Cover Design By:
Val Walderzak, valwalder@gmail.com

Disclaimer: The author and publisher have utilized their best efforts in preparing the information in this book. The stories in this book have been told to us as each woman's experiences and recollections.

Table of Contents

Foreword

Share your truth.

This is what I encourage survivors of intimate partner terrorism (not domestic violence, no – "domestic" waters it down) to do.

I survived two bullets that were intended to end my life. My abusive ex-husband ambushed me at my apartment and shot through the door. My father and I were pushing against the door to keep him out. My young son, age 4, was standing just behind us. I was shot. My dad was shot. My son saw the whole thing. Any of those bullets could have killed one of us, two of us, all of us.

Three generations of one family almost completely wiped out.

But that wasn't our fate. That wasn't how it went for us. We all lived. And because I'm still here, I share my truth. I vowed from my hospital bed that I would tell what happened, in all the messy details, in all the discomfort, as often as I could, in as many places and platforms as possible.

Because what happened wasn't my fault. Abuse isn't our fault. The fault is on the abuser and that is the truth. We need an entire shift in how we talk about the bad things violent offenders do to their partners. The blame and shame should not be carried by victims – the shame is squarely on the shoulders of those who abuse.

The power for change lies within the voices of those of us who made it through, who fought, who persevered in the face of unimaginable horror. We know what it's like to be drowning, barely able to keep our heads from being pulled under the current of the wrath of an abuser. We know – and that's why it's so important to expose it. It can be scary. It can hurt to go back there. It can leave you feeling vulnerable and it can re-open wounds. But you know what? It can also let other women know they aren't alone.

#SheWins 2 and the women who have come forward in this book, clear a path for other women to do the same. When we pull each other up, when we build upon the truths of our lived experiences – when we roar as one to put men and society on notice that no, this isn't okay and we are shining a light on it – that is when lives will be saved.

Share your truth. Take back your power.

Kate Ranta
Co-Author of *Killing Kate*

Introduction

Alisa Divine

She called me out.

Yet, looking back, I just wasn't ready. Healing is composed of many layers and my wound was still raw. Even though I had been divorced for six years at the time I published *#SheWins*, the shrapnel was still under my skin.

I recognized it when *#SheWins* was rated in the Independent Book Publishers Association Benjamin Franklin Awards, one of the highest national honors in independent publishing. One of the three judges awarded it all 10s out of 10.

I welcomed the positive feedback from the first judge who told me what I did right. "TIE BREAKER = #2 WOW WOW WOW — so well done! Excellent cover - excellent pictures used to connect the humanness of abuse and survival! Great text font - The mix and balance of beautiful photography and the stories of each woman will inspire others to realize their value and know they CAN move forward! Just perfect......" ~Judge A

And then I read this: "I would like to know the author's story. She is a survivor, so why did she choose to do this book? What is her own personal connection to how she got the idea for this project? I am left wondering and wanting to know more before she jumps into the stories of the other ladies." ~Judge B

Sometimes we get the greatest takeaways from loss. The judge that gave lower ratings, bumping me out of the winner's circle, was the one who inspired me to follow up with *#SheWins 2*. I felt ready to answer the call. To be more. To do more. To say more.

I'll explain the easy part first — I chose to bring forth *#SheWins* and now *#SheWins 2* to encourage women to speak up and share their stories. Domestic violence thrives in secrecy. We take away its power when we talk about it. When we share our stories. When we move beyond shame and secrecy to freedom and healing.

The women who have shared their stories for this book are change makers. Each one of them has repurposed their pain to create platforms to help others. They advocate, they lead, they teach and they also have transformed their own lives. Domestic violence is far from a glamorous subject. It's not easy to dig into the past, recall trauma and be seen as vulnerable. But this is exactly what these women have done — because they know the reward of transformation. They have identified their strengths and their purpose. And their hope is to inspire others to transformation as well.

I remember sitting on my sofa in April 2018, after one of many issues with the father of my children, thinking — if I could just help one woman with what I went through, maybe everything would have been worth it. Months later, I took inspired action on an idea to photograph women in black and white, showing the emotions of the abuse and even more importantly, showing colorful portraits of women today as strong and empowered in the "after." The book began to take on a life of its own.

What I didn't know was that the evolution of that personal project would shift the trajectory of my own life. I set out to help other women tell their stories. And I did and at times I shared pieces of my story. But I was still living with sadness and shame from one piece that kept me from sharing my story in the first book.

The time has arrived to dig to a deeper level. To begin a new phase of healing from my abusive 18-year relationship. To diminish the power it has held over me.

The time has come to release the piece I've been holding back.

I know you're tired but come,
this is the way.

~ Rumi

Alisa Divine from Michigan
Photographed by Trish Hadley

The Battles I Lost and
The War I Won

I've found screaming at the top of my lungs to be remarkably therapeutic.

When I'm alone. In my bedroom or in the shower. One summer day, I even realized the sliding glass door was open, sorry neighbors! Or I drive down an abandoned road, turn off my car, grip the steering wheel and scream until my throat is sore.

Almost three decades of wounds run deep.

For years, I was the stay-at-home mom that made working moms want to throw up. Or so my daughter's first grade teacher said when I brought in Thanksgiving Day cookies in 2002. They were sugar cookies with white frosting and a maple nut goodie cut in half for the turkey. Mini green M&Ms for peas. A dollop of frosting for the mashed potatoes with a little bit of yellow food gel for the gravy.

I perfected motherhood. And baking and cooking. And laundry. And art projects. And carpooling. And running the backend of his business. I had five kids over 14 years and I did it mostly by myself. He spent the majority of his time either working or drinking. I was a licensed teacher who stayed at home full time, my two oldest had excellent grades and were in advanced classes. My daughter graduated high school with 12 college credits in her pocket. My kids were so well behaved strangers would comment to me about them. One young man who sat near us on the plane even wrote me a letter praising me as a parent when we traveled to Florida. Being a mom was something I was really good at. And having kids was how I felt loved.

I was perfect at holding it all together.

Until 2012 when I finally realized it wasn't sustainable and I filed for divorce.

While watching a Disney movie last summer with my kids, I was reminded how abuse lingers long past the final signatures and stamped divorce papers. *In The Last Song*, there is a divorced mom and dad. The mom was dropping off the kids to the dad. They talked, laughed and then embraced in a hug before the mom left. "Of course Disney would show that version," I thought to myself.

Then my youngest daughter asked, "Wait — are they married?"

My teen answered, "No, they are divorced."

My youngest replied, "And they're nice to each other???"

Yep — we are that family. The one that others talk about, the high-conflict divorcees.

Flashbacks came to me of the judge shaming us in court. "Do you two talk to each other about your kids?"

"No, we can't talk to each other," I said.

The judge went on, "If you two hate each other so much, you can't even talk about your kids..."

He was missing important pieces though. And at the time, I didn't have the words to articulate. Nor the balls to speak up.

Today, I strongly believe that significant changes in family court are necessary.

Today, if I could eliminate one statement from all divorce discussions, it would be this: "If you can just get along for the sake of the children, it's so much better for everyone."

That is a common misconception. In an abusive relationship — there is no such thing as ending with "getting along." The premise of abuse is control and domination over another. Leaving is the most dangerous time for a woman because the man has lost the control he once had over her. It is theoretically impossible for an abusive relationship to end peacefully.

What I managed to relay to my daughter after the Disney movie was this — "Yes, sometimes people who are divorced get along. And then there are situations when they do not. And it's OK for parents to not get along at times because it means they are standing up for what they believe in." I have learned to cultivate my gift of articulation. Part politically correct if viewed in the eyes of the court, no negativity towards her father. Part empowering for a little girl to know she gets to stand up for herself. We need to teach girls there is more to becoming women than sitting still and looking pretty.

> *I spent 18 years "trying" to get along for the sake of the five children we had together because I used to believe that was the "best for everyone."*

I was used to putting everyone else's needs and wants before my own. And I was wrong thinking it was best for my kids for us to stay together. They saw it. They heard it. They cried. I got to the point where staying — was the worst thing for my family.

The judge also was wrong when he said that we hate each other. I don't personally hate my children's father. I hate his behavior. And there is a difference.

I hate that he attacked me at my best friend's wedding in Rhode Island and my life flashed before my eyes. I hate that he dumped all my makeup and my high heels into the toilet. I hate that he damaged hundreds of dollars in our hotel room. I hate that he shit inside my suitcase. I hate that all of my belongings were ruined and I went home wearing my friend's shoes and the shirt off her back, literally. I hate that he harassed me on the flight home when I changed my seat and my friend's big brother had to call the flight attendant to get him to leave me alone. I hate that I still wanted to hide it but my best friends saw it all.

I hate that he discouraged me from finishing my master's degree. I hate that he never wanted me to make money in my photography business. I hate that he wanted me dependent on him. I hate that he told me that I was the one who wanted five kids and so I needed to stay home and take care of them.

4

I hate that because I filed for divorce, drew my boundaries and stood up for myself after 18 years of trying to make it work — that I was accused of hate. THAT was the most loving act I ever did for myself in my life. I hate that I was accused of "not trying," being unreasonable, insensitive and a bitch because he was "so sad" over the divorce, yet he never cleaned up his side of the street.

I hate that he made me sign papers outside of our attorneys' offices to manipulate me. I hate that my first attorney made me fire her because of that.

I hate that he asked me, "Who's ever going to want you? You've had five kids."

I hate that I thought about how many pills I could take to not wake up in the morning because he badgered me and harassed me continually. I didn't know how I would ever get away from him or how I would ever have a normal life.

I hate that I had an alarm installed in my new home because I feared him and had reason to believe he got into my house.

I hate that he refused to sign the divorce papers for six months after the judge awarded the divorce. Only because he would not pay the kids' health insurance and wanted me to go on Medicaid instead — to induce shame I'm sure. Instead, I took on the cost of health insurance and refused Medicaid even after 12 years of being a stay -at-home mom. I cannot believe our divorce stalled for six months because he didn't get what he wanted — me going on Medicaid.

I hate that he took me on a wild goose chase when my grand-mother passed away, refusing to drop off the kids to me at my predetermined parenting time. He drove two hours to the funeral, where he was not welcome. We were divorced! He showed up with the kids in time for the opening prayer. And I was late. Because four or more times he said, "meet me here," "now meet me there," "no there." The kids called me crying saying, "dad won't stop and meet you." And I showed up frantic, missing the opening prayer. And there he was sharing his sympathies with my family while refusing to co-parent with any integrity.

I hate that he put his hands around my neck and choked me and our oldest ran screaming up the stairs carrying our toddler with the other two kids running behind her. I hate that I held the phone in my hand, lying on the bathroom floor afterwards, too scared to call 911 because I knew they would make me leave. I was pregnant with my fifth child and I didn't know how I would take care of myself, four kids and a baby on the way. I hate that he got away with it.

I hate that he volunteers at the school fun fair and donates to places in need and holds friends' little babies — then he chokes his wives behind closed doors. Yes, wives.

I hate that he was abusive to his second wife too.

I hate that the potential third wife is getting love bombed right now. I hate that I have felt responsibility for not speaking up sooner and preventing other women from his abuse.

I hate that it took his second divorce for people to say — "Maybe Alisa is telling the truth." "Maybe Alisa wasn't exaggerating." "Maybe he does put on an act when others are watching." "Maybe Alisa was right in cutting off all communication with him because it ALWAYS has to be his way and his way only."

I hate that my kids see a charming man, who dresses nicely, lives in a big house, with money — who is abusive to women and they may normalize that, or even find a partner like him. I hate that they are at risk by proxy.

I hate that anything I suggested on parenting our kids, he has rejected. I had to learn to let go of what I established as a mother on healthy eating, bedtime routines, impeccable manners, priority on homework and grades, all of which I highly valued and influenced when I was with the kids daily. He has no respect for anything I established with the children.

I hate that he attacked my motherhood. When I think about it — that was all he had left. I had cut off all communication with him and it was court-ordered at that. And there was a court order to only exchange the kids in a public setting because he threatened me, harassed me, or hit my windshield. I drew every boundary so he could not get to me anymore.

And then he did the unfathomable.

The behavior I hate the most — the most gut-wrenching battle of all that I lost — is that the father of my children chose to alienate our son from me. Parental Alienation (PA) (often planned and malicious) is when a parent takes steps to isolate a child from the other parent through words and conduct used to create a division, estrangement and even hostility between the victimized parent and child.

> *It happened so fast that I didn't even realize what was going on until it was out of control. Parental alienation is control, it is abuse.*

When we were married, I never questioned my motherhood. I knew who I was as a mom. I lived to be a mother. My son and I had a healthy, loving relationship for the first 12 years of his life. I remember breastfeeding him on the morning of Sept. 11, 2001, as I watched the Twin Towers collapse on the *Today Show*, while squeezing him ever so tightly. I put flour and rice into a water table in the middle of the living room and as a toddler, he would push his tractors through it playing contently for hours.

He was such a loving, kind-hearted boy. So gentle and funny and so sweet and smart. When he was in kindergarten, he knew the curriculum and was unchallenged. I will say that I taught kindergarten before I was a full-time, stay-at-home mom and that gave him an advantage. He tested much higher than average and was in advanced placement from that point on. His memory was also magnificent, especially with numbers. But sadly, out of all five of my kids, he was the most sick. Severe eczema, asthma, allergies, ear infections and I cared for him through all of it, day and night. I advocated for his healthcare endlessly.

When he was a tween, I took him to a Detroit Tigers game and he played the air guitar to "Don't Stop Believin" by Journey during the seventh-inning stretch. A memory I can never escape — we had the best mother-son day.

Then everything changed in 2014, when my (now) husband and I were dating for six months and decided to introduce our kids. We planned a swimming day. Afterwards, their dad heard about it and asked if he could take our son snowmobiling the following weekend during my parenting time. At first I thought it was great. Maybe he is finally stepping up and spending time with him. Everyone is better off and we are getting past the divorce.

Then when my son no longer wanted to come over to my house as usual, I felt really confused. Domestic abuse often begins or escalates at a significant point — engagement, marriage, having a child together, moving in together, etc. In my case, this new form of abuse, through parental alienation, began at the point when my children met my (now) husband.

I believe their father was insecure with the possibility that his children would be in the presence of another man, another father figure. He felt threatened. I believe that once he discovered I was dating, any thoughts of regaining control over me again, even though we were divorced, were lost. Consciously or unconsciously, the smear campaign against me began. Oddly, this behavior was only directed towards our son, not our four daughters. And in a sick and twisted way, our son became my replacement. He became the new victim of his father's control.

My son quickly became angry at me. And children are not naturally angry, it is a learned behavior. It escalated so fast that his sisters were afraid and crying. He damaged things. He made serious threats. I had to call the police. And some of the details I am choosing to keep private. All of it followed with his father taking me to court saying our son didn't want to be with me. He was rewarded with more parenting time because of the intensity of our son's behaviors.

The reasoning, however, was weak and frivolous. I didn't have a big backyard. He couldn't ride his dirt bike at my house. He was in a house with all females. I pleaded with the judge to change his court-ordered therapist, who had testified in the trial, his male chauvinistic rhetoric showing through.

The judge responded to me with, "Do you have a degree in psychology?"

And I said, "No, I have a degree in education." And he said, "Then no, his therapist stays as is." As if I was not qualified to ask for a change in therapy without a degree in psychology! It was all an unbelievable mess!

I knew the mom I was. I knew the love I had for my son and the love he had for me. None of it made sense and it brought me to my knees.

I began questioning myself. The shame of being erased out of my son's life was intolerable. And that is exactly what it was — an erasure of my existence, my value, my worthiness as a mother, and the validity of all decisions I made on my son's behalf.

> *I began educating myself on parental alienation.*
> *By having some sort of knowledge of it, I knew*
> *what I was feeling and experiencing*
> *was legitimate, felt empowering.*

I wrote letters to my son, all of which I kept — every time I missed his birthday, a holiday or when I felt the unbearable ache of feeling dead to him. My God, it felt like death to me too. And the alienation extended to my entire side of the family, me being the main target.

In the nine years since our divorce, my son never took a vacation with me. The reduced parenting time dwindled to two days per month, then stopped altogether. The actuality is — I'm an adult. I have resources. My brain is fully developed. I've had therapists over the years to help and guide me. I write, I advocate, both of which have helped me to feel empowered. He was a child. Today, in legal terms he is an adult. But he didn't have the same resources and development. His father wanted to hurt me. And he accomplished that. But do you know who he hurt more? Our son. He is the real victim. His father valued control and domination over the well-being and happiness of his own son.

My son's behavior wasn't normal. Children don't reject their parents. Even in cases of child abuse, the child often wants to remain with the abusive parent. So in my case, being the mother that I know I have been for 25 years now, there was no explanation for my son's alienation from me other than his father orchestrated it. I don't know exactly how he did this. I only know what happened. Healthy fathers encourage their children to show love, affection and respect toward their mothers. Our son could have had the best of both worlds — two families with double the love and the experiences.

So before saying, "If you can just get along for the sake of the children, it's so much better for everyone," realize there may be more to the story. One of the best gifts my kids received when their father and I divorced was seeing their mother become a strong-ass woman. I would not be half the woman I am today if my goal was to "get along." To do that, I would have had to concede to his continuous control. I would have had to agree to go on Medicaid, among numerous other suggestions. To "get along" I would have had to do only what he wanted. Instead I fought for what I believed in. I stood up for myself and I spoke out.

Our story is a long, complicated one. We began dating as teenagers and I didn't know much about healthy relationships, let alone toxic relationships. In high school in the 90s, he bought me a Gucci watch with all the different colored rings. I thought that was love. He always had money — which prompted me to turn my head when his 100-hour work weeks were the norm. Or buy his excuses when we were newly married and he went out with the guys Friday nights and never came home until the next day.

He was used to getting away with everything.

He crashed his truck after a night of drinking in high school and his mom took the blame — she said it was her. He got in a fight and his dad went with me to pick him up and told me not to give him a hard time. There was always an excuse or lie or alligator tears that he would change. But he never changed. He never took responsibility for any of it.

The first time I left him, we had been married for a year. I was 22 and we had a three-year old daughter. I also was pregnant. He was so full of anger and rage all the time and that was not a secret. I couldn't live with it anymore. My parents came over to help move me into my grandmother's empty house. He came home and realized what was happening and he lost it — on everyone. My parents told me not to go back to him so I met with an attorney and I filed for divorce. I had a taste of living on my own as a single mom. I remember thinking about my possibilities in life and I felt excited. And then I had a miscarrage. I was weak. He saw the opening. He wrote me a letter. He told me how he would change, how he would be different, that he loved me and our daughter. I dropped the divorce and went back with him. But his actions never matched his words — a lesson that would take me 13 more years to learn.

I went back because I was 22. According to the National Coalition Against Domestic Violence, women between the ages of 18 and 24 are most likely to be in a domestic violence relationship.

> *I stayed because I thought he could change.*
> *I stayed because he told me he would change.*
> *I stayed because I wanted a family more than*
> *anything else in the world.*

 I stayed because my priest told me to forgive him. I stayed because my gynecologist told me that men make mistakes sometimes when he gave me a STD. I stayed because his mom told me that he just needed help. I stayed when my first of many therapists tried to help me realize that he was lying and I couldn't see it. I stayed because I wanted him to be a good person.

After the choking incident and the birth of my fifth child, I didn't consciously make a choice to leave, however I began doing things for myself. I was a blogger and I began learning photography to add photos to my writing. My youngest was 8 weeks old, sleeping through the night and I stayed awake devouring photography tutorials, Photoshop lessons and finding forums online with other photography moms. I filed a Doing Business As (dba) and I started charging people to take their pictures.

He told me I didn't "need" to make money doing it, I should just do it for free — I charged anyway. He told me I couldn't take our youngest two children to daycare to work on my photography business while the older kids were in school — I did it anyway. I began to do the things I wanted to do whether he liked it or not. I traveled by myself and went to photography conferences. I met with a lawyer to file for divorce and then I backed out. I went to training to lead a mission trip to Costa Rica. I found a new therapist and began to realize by staying, I was doing more harm to my family than good.

Then I hired the lawyer again, consulted my therapist and made a plan. We all knew there was no way in hell he wouldn't put up a fight. But after the initial shock of being served, he appeared to handle it surprisingly well. He began spending time with the kids and he wanted to "agree" on everything. He really wanted 50/50 custody and even though I had the advantage of being a stay-at-home mom and could have had sole physical custody, I wanted to do the "right" thing and give him a chance to be the dad he said he wanted to be. He said we could "sign" some papers out of court to "agree" on things. He played me for a fool. After I agreed to what he wanted, he became unagreeable. My lawyer advised me against signing anything without her and when I didn't listen she refused to represent me further. I had to hire a new lawyer and start over.

Even though I could have taken half of everything from the house, I didn't. I tried multiple times to get my things that were awarded in the divorce settlement and each time it was a shit show. When I called the police, they asked me to leave and come back when he was less upset. But there would never be a time when he was less upset. Manipulation was the name of the game. And after months of this, I said, "Fuck it. It's only stuff." And I never got any of it — my grandmother's hand-sewn quilt, the kids' baby books, their grade school memorabilia I saved and more. It was another example of him using the kids as a weapon to punish me for leaving.

I saw time spent arguing with him further was time not spent on rebuilding my life. So I dove into my photography business through online courses and forums. I focused on photographing women, high school seniors, corporates and portraits. I set a goal to have 30-50 photo shoots in a year and if I did, I would reward myself with a photo shoot of my dreams, with mentor Sue Bryce. And the following year, I flew to Los Angeles to achieve that. In turn, that led to working with a cohort of female photographers meeting with Sue in LA over the next year. I was beginning to see that I had the power to create my reality and live my dreams.

I met my (now) husband on a blind date, set up by my sister and his long-time friend. I opened a photography studio in his hometown. I established myself in a new city and built a network near and far. We got married, moved in together and blended our family of 10, which makes me incredibly proud.

The support he has shown me has been endless through all the twists and turns we never saw coming. Some of my experiences broke me, as you can imagine. My husband didn't always have the answers or know what to say, but he has been by my side through everything – even at times when I pushed him away, not having enough experience trusting a man. And yet he remained strong and steady, picking me up off my knees or lying next to me while I cried. All the while allowing me space to heal those pieces with time. I am grateful for the loving man he is.

Along the way I founded The *More Than Beautiful Project*™, when I saw the need while working with teens and women to develop greater confidence, build healthy relationships and maintain positive mindsets. I taught several rounds of the program and now have it available as an online course on my website. It is literally everything I wish I would have known to prevent me from being and staying in an abusive relationship.

Be the person you needed when you were younger.
That is what The More Than Beautiful Project™ *is to me.*
What I believe all women need to know.

As I continued my "new life," I submerged myself into self-development courses, worked with business coaches, and continued building. Then I met a woman at my studio who told me she worked with our local domestic violence shelter, helping women write their stories of overcoming. It was at the same time I had an idea to do a series of black and white photographs. I knew I was onto something — photographing women and telling their stories of abuse. How they overcame to become strong and empowered. I made one move, asking an acquaintance in publishing if he would be interested in my book idea. He said "yes." That eventually led to me becoming part of the publishing company, and today I am CEO. I also joined the Board of Directors of the local domestic violence shelter.

Publishing that first book, *#SheWins,* which received acclaim as a finalist in the Next Generation Indie Book Awards, led to more writing and less photography. I closed my studio and chose to write and publish full time. Then came another book, Award Winner and Amazon best seller, *Killing Kate,* and another Amazon #1, *She Rises.*

Through those deeply personal book projects, something happened. I became more articulate through hundreds of speaking events, podcasts and interviews about the books, and domestic violence. I became more brave telling pieces of my story. Women all over reached out to me, thanking me. Women in their 60s and 70s confided in me that they had never shared their experiences of domestic violence until they told me.

> *When one woman tells her story, it gives permission*
> *to other women to do the same.*
> *It's powerful.*

In the beginning of 2021, I filed a motion in the court for a change in custody. I wrote the motion by myself and I represented myself. I had considered the motion for the last eight years and my divorce lawyer didn't think I would be favored. Others agreed and so I stalled. But my pain became the flame that set my soul on fire. I could not write this story knowing there was more I could do. I made the decision based on what felt right to me. It wasn't about winning, it was about standing up for what I believe in. So I hand-picked five of the Michigan Child Custody Act factors and I wrote an eight-page motion detailing the ways in which the father of my children violated those factors.

Keep in mind, custody had been established almost a decade earlier and was unlikely to change. However, it got the attention of a new judge, as our divorce judge retired. A hearing was set. The judge said my motion warranted further investigation and progressed to mediation.

I began to feel heard and validated for the first time in years. The presence of domestic violence was acknowledged and prior to mediation I answered a domestic violence screening form — none of which occurred through the divorce and first custody trial. And I believe Renee, whose story is also in this book, helped establish this crucial step through her work with the Bay County Friend of Court. We are all intertwined in this evolution of society. Mediation was held separately, due to the answers on the domestic violence screening. The mediator told me "congratulations, you have accomplished a great deal on your own. I read your motion and these issues need to be addressed." The mediator recommended our case move on to investigation, which will likely progress to a trial. Since, I have decided to hire a new attorney to feel fully supported through his expertise and guidance.

I lost many battles but regardless of the outcome to be determined within the court system, I have won the war. Piece by piece, I turned all of the pains I endured into power to fuel my life and help more women do the same.

I listened to my intuition to file the motion. I held faith that everything was working in my favor — even when it didn't look like it. I took my power back. I stood up and spoke out. I said these behaviors are unacceptable and changes need to be made. I can no longer sit by with the knowledge, the articulation and the domestic violence experience I have today. The court system began to listen to me. This is significant because although there was physical violence during our marriage, it was more than nine years ago and invalid in the current case. My case is based on the most difficult behaviors to prove — control, domination and manipulation, all of which are difficult to see. By shining a light on it, I know domestic abuse cannot thrive in exposure.

As I write this, I am addressing my relationship with my son with my therapist and doing what I can to heal the wound. The wound was not my fault, nor my son's fault and I'm taking responsibility for the healing and reconnection. I'm ready to have the difficult conversations and open the new doors.

When I answered the call to produce this book, I never imagined how much my decision to write my own story would become a catalyst for even deeper healing and clearing in my life. If you really want to heal at a level you've never experienced yet, write your story and share it with others.

Through my process I felt a need to address everything that felt unsettled within me. Healing is layers. It wasn't easy, but it was transformative and as a result, I now feel an even louder calling to BE more of the leader that I've always known is within me.

My story may never be done — but the war is over.

I have peace in my soul.

I have decided, #SheWins!

*A good father does not abuse his children's mother.
A man's abuse of a mother proves in itself that he
is not thinking or caring adequately about
what is good for the children.*

~ Lundy Bancroft

Staci Austin from Texas
Photographed by
Michelle Loconto

The First Wife

Internal affairs investigation of family violence 10-0329-0017 was not a police report filed by my husband, a Texas police officer.

It was filed **against** him.

I was taught by my teachers and family that policemen kept us safe and I believed that through many years of my life...until 2009.

This is where my story begins. My name is Staci Austin, and I am 43, the mother of three boys ages 25, 20 and 12. I live and work as a realtor in the Austin, Texas area. In 2005, I thought I had figured it all out — a single mom of two boys going into real estate. I was ready to kill it financially. The only concern I had was passing the state and national real estate exams. I received my real estate license in 2006 and earned the title of "Rookie of The Year" at Coldwell Banker the same year. I purchased a new house, saved some money, sported a new red BMW, and had zero credit cards. The options in life were almost as open as the day I graduated high school.

I purchased my second home in a matter of two years of being a licensed realtor. My boyfriend and I had been together for about four years and I had a plethora of friends that I hung out with all the time. I admit that I was not the most attentive mother, but my boys were well taken care of and I tried my best at such a young age.

However, I am a woman who loves too hard. I have exhausted myself and have recently concluded that I always see the best values in others. Now I realize that this is a flaw. I admit to being an overly friendly person that people tend to take advantage of. It has got me into trouble from time to time. I am entirely too trusting, and currently reaping the repercussions. My counselor and I are working on this behavior. I am a narcissist magnet. Maybe it is due to my smile and sincere, kind heart. I truly just care and want to help people.

Why do guys think that a smile means that you are interested in them? Anyway... a police officer sounded amazing to this single mom in 2007. A protector, stable job, loves kids, health insurance, protects, serves and is giving.

Sounded great after supporting my boyfriend who did not want to get married. Who knew that I would find a guy that seemed to have all those great qualities just months after my breakup and that he would ask me to marry him after only three months of dating?

I met him for the first time at the HEB grocery store, in Round Rock, Texas on HWY 79. I was just making my weekly grocery run with my son Collin, who was in the shopping cart. I was approached by a man wearing athletic shorts and a t-shirt in the meat department. OMG, the meat department, seriously!!!? He approached me asking, "Do I know you from somewhere?" I said that I wasn't sure, and I asked if he was a realtor. I did not think anything other than that he was hitting on me. He then sent an email wanting to get together through my Coldwell Banker site. I was not interested in dating him because I was in a relationship with my boyfriend who was living with me at that time.

A few weeks after the HEB incident, I remember seeing a Round Rock police officer several times in the neighborhood. I lived in a small subdivision in a cul-de-sac, the first house as you turned in. There was only one way in and one way out and most of the windows of my house faced that entrance. I did not realize at the time that the police officer patrolling my neighborhood was the guy I met at the grocery store. My two boys were coming home from school one day when the police officer stopped his car, waved at me, and said, "Hi, I am just doing my rounds to make sure your neighborhood is safe." I also remember seeing him in Round Rock at the YMCA parked next to my car. That was strange, to say the least.

Now, I regret that I was not more suspicious of him.

Months later, I made a 911 call about a person attempting to break into my house. This incident involved a mentally ill man that lived across the street. The man would stare me down often and had strange behaviors that made the boys and me uncomfortable.

At one point he tried to open the front door of my home. When the police arrived at the scene, I remember seeing them tackling the guy down in the front yard. The same Round Rock cop that patrolled my neighborhood asked me to write a statement of what happened. I still did not recognize him as the man who approached me at the grocery store.

He called me days after the incident to say that he lost my report and needed to come to my house to have me write up another statement. As I was writing up my second statement, he wanted to know if I remembered him from the grocery store.

I started putting two and two together.

He mentioned that he noticed that the guy who owned the blue truck was not staying at my house anymore. I told him that the blue truck belonged to my boyfriend, but we broke up and he recently moved out.

The officer wanted to know if I would ever be interested in a date with him. I do not remember exactly what I said that night, but I remember thinking it was an odd statement. Nonetheless, I was flattered. He was tall, dark, and handsome but I was going through a breakup and was not really interested at that particular moment. He called me a few times after that and I never met up with him but oddly kept running into him. He appeared at some of the same restaurants where I was eating and he continued patrolling the neighborhood.

Then he pulled me over one night while I was driving. I was heading home and about a block away when he noticed that I did not have a front license plate on my car. He just wanted to say "hi" in my opinion and had an excuse to pull me over. We chatted a bit and I remember him saying, "You know that it's a 'God thing' that we keep running into each other." I saw him more and more frequently around the neighborhood and our chats got longer and longer until I agreed to take a ride in his patrol car.

Beluga Japanese Restaurant was the location of our first date. I was incredibly happy and excited. I still remember the butterflies in my stomach while waiting. When he arrived to pick me up, he acted extremely nervous and I remember thinking it was cute. He said that he did not date very often and he was surprised that someone like me would even consider a date with him. He was friends with whom I thought to be the owner of Beluga, but he could have been just a waiter. He surprised us with all kinds of sushi including an Ahi Tuna Tower, which was my favorite. My first red flag that I overlooked was when he stepped away to the bathroom.

The waiter said, "you don't want to date this guy."
These words still haunt me.

We saw each other daily from that point on and I found myself falling head over heels for him right away. His charm and passion for me made me overlook some strange behaviors. He was an intense lover and had a passion that I had never experienced. He did get too intense at times and I had to stop him when he began physically hurting me with his body. In one instance he squeezed handcuffs on me that caused my wrists to bruise.

He started staying at my house every night and around the three month mark, he got on his hands and knees on my bedroom floor and asked me to marry him. He gave me a ring that had three amazing diamonds and I thought it was beautiful! I was so excited, yet very surprised. I also could not believe that he wanted to marry me so quickly.

I wanted to have a big white wedding with all our friends and family but he was adamant about getting married at the courthouse. I found out that I was pregnant not long after that and so we married at the Williamson County Courthouse on May 27, 2008. I continued to plan my big white wedding for August 2008. My dress had been previously altered and I was worried because I knew that my belly was only going up in size.

Once married, he disclosed several things that made me seriously question him. He said that when he met me at HEB, he followed me out to my car in the parking lot and wrote down my license plate number. He also stated that after my 911 call, he recognized my address and told the dispatcher that he was going to take the call even though it was out of the area he was assigned to patrol. He went out of his district a lot because he wanted to get to know me. He also admitted that he never lost the statement that I wrote regarding the mentally ill man, even though he told me he did.

Within weeks of our marriage, he wanted me to end my career in real estate and refused to pay the renewal to keep my license current. He said that real estate was not safe and I needed to be at home more with my boys. I took a job working at Lancome at Macy's selling makeup. Although I enjoyed working there, I felt at times like an idiot going to my little hourly-paying job with a truly small commission. That was difficult for me after making great money selling homes.

My self-esteem was slowly falling through the cracks. He would call me a "bitch," "whore" and "slut" when he was angry and told me how stupid I was. I started doing things out of character to try to make him happy, like cooking more frequently. On one occasion we had a fight and he threw all my sexy lingerie, tight fitted shirts and some high heels in the trash can outside. He said, "You wore them for other men!" He even ripped some of my clothes with his hands. For some reason I began to believe that maybe I was wrong for having sexy lingerie or wearing tops that showed a little cleavage. He would also say, "You are a Mommy, and you need to dress like a Mommy!" He took me to Old Navy to show me which "Mommy clothes" to purchase. He also became enraged over things like if I spent too much time at the gym or if I simply spoke to any man for any reason.

I began to get paranoid about little things that might make him mad and would rush to get home from places.

Often he would show up at my place of business unannounced and I thought it was sweet in the beginning, not knowing that he was there watching me. Eventually, I was pulled into the office by my employer telling me an employee complained about him making a scene and said that he made her nervous to leave work at night. She asked me to explain. I really think he was trying to get me fired.

My friends began to either go away or distance themselves because he would make them extremely uncomfortable or intentionally make them upset. One incident occurred when a close friend was on her way to my bridal shower when she got pulled over. She told the Round Rock police officer my name, that I was marrying a fellow officer and she was headed to my bridal shower. He radioed to my fiance and she heard him tell the officer to ticket her. She later told me about the ticket.

> *His fits of rage started happening more and more frequently. He would snap and start punching walls and doors, throwing and breaking furniture.*

He broke computers and phones to destroy evidence. He kicked down a portion of the fence and ripped up plants and flowers that he planted in the front and backyards. He would punch and kick his German Shepard named Gordy if he went pottty in the house. He would throw my boys down to the floor when he was angry at them for menial things and at times held or locked us in closets. I stated once that I was going to call the police during a rage. He went into the closet, grabbed one of his guns, placed it to his head and said, "do it." I spent many nights cuddled up with the boys on a twin bed. I was not able to sleep, terrified and in protection mode.

During my pregnancy, I gained barely 15 to 20 pounds. I remember my doctor asking me if I had been eating enough during my third trimester. I was miserable both mentally and physically and my self-esteem was shot. Some of my coworkers were overly concerned for me because I was not the same vibrant girl that used to show up at work. I was a nervous wreck and to some degree I feared for my life. At one point, he grabbed me by my arms and roughly lifted me off my feet, ramming my back into the kitchen counter. It shook me up badly and caused a line bruise along my back. I went to the doctor to make sure the baby was ok the next day. He made sure he was with me for that particular appointment.

Landon was born on March 26, 2009 at Seton Williamson Hospital in Round Rock, TX. He was the prettiest baby that I had ever seen. I was worried about him watching the birth because he said that he could never look at me in a sexual way again if he saw the baby come out of me. He was actually in a wonderful spirit the day of Landon's birth up until his sister and her husband wanted to drive up and see their new nephew. He got really angry and told them not to come when they were on their way. I still can't understand why. Weeks later, I found out that my dear friend Charmaine came to the hospital and he told her to leave.

As the months went by, the mental and physical abuse escalated. On the night of Super Bowl 2010, all of us went to my parents' house to watch the game. I was having a hard time getting my oldest boy Jacob to do his homework. He was being disrespectful to me on the way home. Jacob said, "stop being a bitch" and my ex went into a rage. He drove fast and crazy to the following street. I remember a fence on both sides, where no one could see. He opened the back passenger door and grabbed Jacob by his hair, throwing him roughly to the ground. His head hit the pavement. It was as if Jacob were a criminal resisting arrest and he had him pinned down. He screamed, "I will hurt you kid! Don't you test me!" My three boys were hysterically crying. I was terrified, in shock and my ears were ringing. He was in a rage and my response was to stay calm.

I didn't call the police right away because I was in fear of our lives. I remained as calmly as possible because I didn't want to escalate a bad situation to worse. Days later, Jacob told me that he had an indentation on his head that happened as a result of hitting the pavement when my ex threw him to the ground. He was also complaining of headaches and was missing a patch of hair. I indeed felt a concave surface and observed an absence of hair on the right side of his head. I immediately booked an appointment with his pediatrician. Jacob and I told him the horrific details involving the incident and he ordered a CT scan. This pediatrician was later subpoenaed to a grand jury court trial involving my ex and this case. There was and still remains today an indentation on the right side of Jacob's skull that is visible when he shaves his head.

I was looking for ways out many times. I was done, yet I felt trapped.

I was broken and yet my ex's world was starting to crumble. His dad suddenly died and then his 28-year-old sister passed as well. I felt something for this man, which is not an excuse for staying.

Another incident occurred when he was lying on the bed with the baby. I said something that triggered him into a rage and he lunged from the bed, grabbed my throat and strangled me to the floor. I thought he was going to kill me. His eyes were wide and crazy. I could not breathe and began to black out. When I came to, my ears were ringing and I remember Landon being face down on the floor screaming. I grabbed Landon and ran out the front door into the greenbelt. I remember feeling numb, it was almost like it was not reality. When I returned, I told him that I was going to call the police and he said, "Go ahead, here let me call them for you and I will show them the scratches you made on me and have you arrested." Not realizing it, I had dug my fingernails into his arms when he was choking me. I did not call the police immediately and did not write a report, therefore I later found out that the incident did not mater to the police investigations.

He was raging more and more and I was helpless, a measly 100 pounds, if that. I finally broke and called 911.

He slapped the phone out of my hand during this occurrence. When they came to my home, they saw all of the destruction that he caused and took photos of all the broken furniture, seven doors, and holes in many walls. As a couple of police officers talked to him outside, another officer remained in the house and told me to get my things and get out. I packed a bag and left my home. It was broken in so many pieces anyway.

I was actually giving in at that point and was asking for help from the police department, as to what to do and…. I was terrified. I can remember the exact location of where I was standing and the look on my sons' faces, Jacob and Collin, while I was talking to the police. I told my sons not to say too much, but they did speak and I found myself spitting out things that I was so terrified to say…I was always threatened by my ex not to talk. He told me that he would shoot me in my sleep with a pillow over my head and that he knew what a 45 tasted like. Those words still haunt me at times today and guns still trigger me.

I moved in with my parents and finally got the courage to file a protective order. He continued to threaten my life if I wrote a statement. I was extremely scared and nervous walking through the Williamson County Courthouse with my short, scared-girl version of the real story. For some reason, I remember a police officer asking if he could record me while asking questions about the application for the protective order. It seemed like the police were against me and I was getting more nervous and scared.

The report said in part:

She said Officer M. had been aggressive and physical with her in the past, and when I asked an approximate duration, she said at least six months. Staci said what finally prompted her to move out and go stay with her parents was an argument which culminated in him putting his hands around her neck and choking her, then pushing her to the ground three times during the course of one argument.

Staci said that he had been physical with her in the past, but that specific incident scared her so badly she felt compelled to leave. Staci also stated that when he has put his hands on her in the past, some instances have left red marks and bruising. Photographs sent from best friend Kellyn....

I contacted an attorney, who agreed to take my case. She told me that police questioning with a tape recorder is "fishy." We withdrew the protective order, filed for a divorce and a restraining order against him immediately. That did not stop him from knocking on my window in the middle of the night, or keeping me from getting inside my vehicle during our meetups on child visitation days.

> **Some of the longest and some of the scariest times in my memory were the visitations involving Landon. When he could no longer abuse me, he abused Landon.**

I began noticing bruises on him when he came home. I took photos of the bruises and reported them to CPS. Landon's preschool director and counselor reported incidents to CPS. He got kicked out of preschool for punching walls and hurting friends.

Then I decided it was time to make a statement.
That police report read in part:

On the morning of 05/28/2010, I received a phone call from Staci. She advised that she was ready to give a statement and wished to cooperate with the investigation. She advised that she had a meeting scheduled with the County Attorney's Office that afternoon in reference to a protective order. Staci refused to meet me at Round Rock PD to give a Statement.

Staci is afraid of him. He has been violent with her on more than one occasion. He has an anger problem. Staci's friend, Kellyn, told Staci to start taking pictures of her injuries and property damage. Staci sent some of the pictures to Kellyn and deleted the rest. In another instance, he was laying in the bed with the baby. Staci and he were arguing, and he lunged from the bed and grabbed her around her throat with his hands. Staci thought he was going to kill her. Staci had red marks after the assult but no other injury.
Supervisor Martinez, M.

I now believe that if I had called the police immediately and written a statement about both of these cases and many more that I have not mentioned, he would have been arrested and found guilty during a grand jury trial. But I was terrified and threatened that he would "take me down" if I ever wrote a statement.

>*It is no wonder why so many abusers with power get off.*
>*An abused woman is scared for her life to call the police,*
>*therefore he gets off??!!! WTF?*

It is not a matter of how many people know the story and believe. It's a matter of filing a police report AT THE EXACT TIME OF OCCURRENCE or the proof is NULL AND VOID!

CPS found that there was "reason to believe" he was abusing the children. My other two boys gave a videotaped deposition at the Williamson County Children's Advocacy Center regarding the incidents involving him throwing Jacob by the hair onto his head which resulted in trauma to his skull.

But despite the CPS findings, multiple statements from different counselors, friends and interviews, photos and medical reports, nothing mattered as much as filing a police report at the EXACT TIME OF OCCURENCE.

Therefore the grand jury failed to indict him. The outcome read:

Internal Affairs Unit of the Round Rock PD reprimanded Officer M. for interfering with other officers 3/1.06.04 and for Unbecoming Conduct 3/1.01.01 in 2010 where the grand jury decided not to indict him for assault because his wife did not provide a written statement on allegations that he beat her. Officer M. was reprimanded again twice in 2013 where the grand jury cleared him of the criminal charges.

It wasn't until my ex found another victim and remarried that justice was in some way served. When he choked his new wife the incident was reported on the TV news because he was a police officer. I was livid that this abuse happened to someone else. His new wife reached out to me and we met in person to talk. I wanted to be a support to her as she went through the legal system.

**Finally she won a judgment against him
when he took a plea bargain.**

Officer M. was arrested and charged with assault by strangulation/ family violence. He made a deal with prosecutors and permanently surrendered his peace officer license for his felony charge in 2016. He also terminated his rights to his son Landon in 2016.

There are still mental and physical scars that affect me and my children. On Aug. 14, 2020, I had nose surgery to correct a deviated septum from when he hit me in the face with a drawer. All three of my children have had their fair share of therapy regarding trauma. Landon still speaks about the times that his father locked him in a dark closet alone, a Buzz Lightyear toy was his only light. His teachers wanted to hold him back for the years of kindergarten and first grade. He suffered from trauma-related stuttering until the third grade. He is currently a happy and healthy sixth grader but will not sleep in the dark.

Today, I am happy and healthy. I still suffer from insomnia and have an occasional bad dream. I am almost completely back to the person I once was, before my abuser in most ways. I have become a stronger person spiritually and mentally. I have learned many valuable life lessons.

I did not talk about my abuse for many years. I am not scared any more. I am not out to get him, I am out to help other women. There are so many victims that don't know it yet. I want people to look at my story and know that this could happen to anyone.

So please pay attention to my important advice:

- Don't be fooled by the quick and charming.
- Pay attention to the red flags.
- Call 911 immediately, tell the entire story to the police AND provide a written statement.
- Don't be terrified of the consequences, they could be much worse if you stay.
- Stop trying to protect the abuser! I still loved the abuser. I didn't want things to be worse if I went back to him. Really?!!
- If you take photos of your bruises, make sure to **include your face** or they won't be part of the investigation.
- The abuser knows what he is doing and sometimes has it planned out before meeting you face to face.
- His intentions may be to squash and rebuild you the way he wants you.
- Listen to your thoughts that tell you to "get out." Stop thinking with your heart and start thinking with your head. Leave your situation, even if it entails leaving all of your personal things. It won't be easy but YOU and YOUR CHILDREN deserve a better place.

Finally, don't count on the police to solve your problem. Ultimately it is what YOU do to correct the situation of your own abuse.

Your choices now may save your children, or the "next woman's" life.

When we deny the story, it defines us. When we own the story, we can write a brave new ending.

~ Brene' Brown

Courtney Petersen from Texas
Photographed by Jenni Roberts

The Second Wife

I love to see women look in the mirror when I am finished doing their makeup. Sometimes they see themselves in a more confident, empowered way. Sometimes they say to me, "I never thought I could look like this." I just tell them, "I enhanced the beauty that always was there." A swipe of lipstick is uplifting and yet cathartic at the same time.

Cosmetics have always been a passion of mine. I worked in the industry for more than 17 years before I started my own cosmetic line. Now I own SPEAK Cosmetics LLC (www.speakcosmetics. com) for a cause, creating a platform for abuse survivors to have a voice and share their stories. Every lip color represents a survivor, real women who shared their story so others know they are not alone. There is hope, there is life on the other side and most importantly there is healing.

Here I am SPEAKing my own story so that others may recognize the signs and take the steps to leave their abuser.

In 2014, I was in a place where I felt confident. I was 34, had a thriving career as a sales trainer for a cosmetic company, traveled frequently and loved what I did. I was on a fitness adventure, working toward competing in my first bodybuilding competition. I was active in my church, volunteering in the mornings and involved in a weekly Bible study. I say all of this to let others know that the women who find themselves in an abusive relationship are not always in a bad place in life. The men who abuse, manipulate, lie and writhe their way into someone's life do a good job playing a version of Dr. Jeckell behind their actual Mr. Hyde.

I met my ex online through a popular dating website. On our first date he was charming, a gentleman, and an incredible listener. He was attentive to everything I said, asking me many questions about my life, my beliefs and he "openly" shared his. We talked about what we wanted for our future, which for both of us was stability and a family. He seemed very open and not secretive, sharing that he had a son and had him every other weekend (which would prove to be a lie, he had not seen him in more than six months). He was so open about his spiritual beliefs yet later I learned they were not his full beliefs. He was creating artificial intimacy in order for me to feel safe, to share my beliefs, my background. But there was still something, something that made my chest uneasy. I mistook that tight feeling for butterflies, for excitement, for a chemical connection.

However, I should have paid more attention to his words and actions.

On our first date I was wearing a hippie headband around my head. In the middle of our date, he took it off and told me, "You are so much prettier without it." It may seem like such a small flag, if any flag at all, but the way he did it said, "you should do what I say." I brushed it off. He hugged me goodbye and we talked about planning another date. I did not hear from him over the next few days, so I reached out to him. After we went out a few more times he told me that he thought he would never see me again. He said his impression of me was that I was confident, educated, beautiful and that I was out of his league. That was all very flattering to me, however down the road he told me I misled him — that he believed me to be this wholesome woman when later he constantly accused me of being a whore.

Our second date was me going on a ride-along with him during his police shift. That evening he asked me to lie about how we met because he did not want others to know that we met online. I laughed this off and still told one of his fellow officers how we met. I could tell this really bothered him. I would come to later find out that he felt that women who were on dating websites were sluts and he did not take them seriously. Yes, you read that correctly. He himself was on this site, dating multiple women and not only on one dating site but several. I also remember him asking me about how I felt about cheating. I did not think it was "ok" to cheat. I look back on how strongly he talked about being faithful in a relationship which would later be so confusing because he cheated on me multiple times.

Our third date took a bit of a different turn. He told me it was the best night he had ever had, making me feel incredibly special. I distinctly remember him telling me that I should not try to change the way I looked (as I was prepping for my bodybuilding competition). If I were to walk down the aisle with him that day with the body I had, he would say he would be the luckiest guy in the world.

I remember these small things because they were hints of the "love bombing." I remember feeling slightly uncomfortable with him mentioning "walking down the aisle." I was thinking, wow this is going way too fast. But at the same time I felt elated. Later I learned he created artificial intimacy to make me feel safe to share details about my own insecurities so he could use them against me.

Three months later he gave me a promise ring. It was his way of sharing his intent to propose to me. But there were several flags that I ignored. During my body building competition, he was very impatient with me because the whole day was about me and my friends who came to watch. He ended up going to a bikini bar next door and missed half of my competition. A month or so later a friend came into town and we were all going to go to dinner. When she brought a date he got angry complaining he had gotten dressed up and bought a new shirt to impress her. We argued. He ended up ripping the shirt because he didn't want the memory of that night when he wore the shirt again. That very thing— ripping his clothes — was something he did several times during our relationship.

Somehow we ended up always getting into an argument when we would meet up with any of my friends.

Typically, it would be because I somehow made him look bad, or the mere fact that I didn't "build him up." That should have been the red flag that made me leave but being on the inside, when we were together, when it was just the two of us, I laughed the hardest, felt the most beautiful and felt like I was more appreciated than I had ever felt. As our relationship developed, I saw my friends less and less because I didn't want to face the repercussions.

In the early stages of our relationship, when he would get angry, there was typically something that would get destroyed — a picture

38

of us, a card that we had given each other, a shirt that "I liked." One night he took my promise ring, got a nickel and etched into it. He was mad that I had seen another guy in our early stages of dating even though I was not aware that he also was dating someone else. Because I had been with someone else he said it left a stain in our relationship and I should be reminded of the stain with the mark in my ring.

Four months into our relationship, I felt my worth starting to be dictated by how this man viewed me.

I started to believe the things he would tell me "in anger" about myself. I even started to inflict pain on myself by scratching my nails into my chest and into my arms as a way I tried to cope. I knew it wasn't healthy but I had never been in such inner turmoil and was trying to show him how deeply he was hurting me. He would point the finger at me to make me feel that this was a sign of my imbalance. Afterwards he would be sorry and try to convince me that was "not the man he really was." I'm here to tell you, listen. Watch what someone says and does. They are always SHOWING you the person they really are.

In April, six months into our relationship, he asked me to marry him. While this should have been a magical moment, it was terrifying for me. The day after he proposed, I found out I was pregnant. I remember how elated and excited he was — we went to the beach and had such a wonderful day. Then, for no apparent reason, he went silent. I knew something was wrong. He then angrily told me how embarrassed he was to have a child with me, that this child had a slut for a mother, that I was nothing but a "cum dumpster" and he didn't want the child to come out of my vagina, the same vagina that had slept with X number of men.

He didn't come out and physically assault me out of nowhere. It started off as verbal, emotional and physiological abuse. That week something in me broke. The rage within him lingered and he verbally assaulted me over and over. I miscarried that following weekend. I felt not only weak physically but also mentally, emotionally and spiritually. I was exhausted from arguing and losing a baby. I spent so much of my time in my car as my escape or in the bathtub with the bathroom door locked.

The fights got worse but so did the regret and pain he felt after. I believed him. I had promised him so many times I would never leave him. I felt I did not have another choice except to make it work and I truly loved him.

The verbal abuse would go in waves. He destroyed anything that he thought represented me being with other men — my purse, my lingerie, two phones and more. Then the tide would change and there would be waves of affection and attention, with ultimate praise. And then crash, another wave would bring me down to a dark, painful place.

The nights that he would break things, so loudly and violently, I was sure someone would call the police. But he would always tell me, "who are they going to listen to? I am the police." We once got into such a bad argument about our "past lives" and how I could never please him like his exes that I threw a vase on the floor. It was the first time I had reacted the way he did. He retaliated by hammering my engagement ring until the diamonds flew everywhere and the band broke. I felt this was a symbol of our relationship. We were broken but could be "fixed" so I had the ring fixed.

***I knew something had to change so I encouraged him
to go to counseling and he agreed.***

At first it seemed to help — there was a calming period and I felt there were breakthroughs within him. Then there was a shift and I became the target of the counseling sessions. He accused me of "triangulating" situations by talking about our relationships to someone outside of us. He would check my phone when I slept, and dig through all of my email and social media if he thought I was talking badly about him.

We got married in September, exactly one year from the day that we met. The wedding was just the two of us at a courthouse. I felt we would be different after marriage — our relationship more secure. But things did not change. He got more sexually demeaning and the arguments grew more violent and physical. The first physical altercation took place when he shoved me into the corner of a door and I cut the back of my head. Afterwards he cried, held me and we went into the closet and prayed. I did not think he would ever lay his hands on me again. But he did.

When I found a book of police reports that his ex-wife filed against him for his violence toward her and her son, he said she made them up. He said they all were investigated and he had not been arrested. I believed him.

How could he still be a police officer
if all of that really happened?

When we got married, I also changed careers after he started traveling with me on almost every trip out of town. At first I thought it was nice that he wanted to have a "get away" with me. Then I realized that he did not trust himself when I was away and he did not trust me. Within one month of getting married, I received a Facebook message from a woman who claimed she had gone on a date with him a couple of weeks prior and she had no idea that he was married.

He had gone out with her after I had fallen asleep one night right when we got married! He calmly did not deny it. He offered me his phone and shared with me that he had been on two different dating sites. He let me look through all his messages to about 30 women. The next day he showed remorse and I forgave him. He bought me 120 long stem roses and to this day I am not a fan of roses.

When we went on a honeymoon to Florida I saw messages to a woman saying he was in Florida on business and wouldn't have access to a phone because he was working SWAT…The lies grew and grew. In the 10 months we were married there would be two more cheating lies I caught but I can't imagine how many there were that I did not catch.

Time passed and I grew more distant from my friends and family. I lived in a constant state of sadness and confusion not knowing which one of his two personalities would show up that day. Then the weekend came that changed the course of my life forever. We

41

got into an argument and I remember driving home from work bracing myself for what I would walk into. He came home a few hours later, said nothing and walked straight over to my work iPad. He broke it over his knee. I was so stunned by this, I remember running to the bedroom saying, "What if I destroyed your work property?" He followed me, grabbed me, flipped me around and wrapped his forearm into my neck putting me in a chokehold. I was desperately trying to break his grip, clawing at his arm, scratching him trying to breathe. That was when he pushed me onto the bed and in that instant I thought I was going to die. I couldn't scream, I could not get a sound out, I couldn't breathe.

The next thing I knew, I was on the floor and passed out. I woke up and saw his face – his eyes were dark with rage. His entire body was tense. Still dizzy, I got up, ran to the bathroom and locked the door. I looked in the mirror and realized I was bleeding. His chokehold forced me to bite my lip as his forearm came up to my neck. I was scared and in shock. I heard him leave the room, so I ran out of the bathroom and out the front door. He was the officer on duty in our apartment complex and many of our neighbors knew this. I was in my pajamas. There were two people that were outside their apartment that I ran past barefooted and yelling "Please GOD." They did not ask if I was ok or if I needed help. I ran to a nearby pond and texted him "give me a reason not to call the police, I bit through my lip, you choked me so hard." He did not respond.

Less than an hour later I walked back to my apartment and saw his truck was gone. I went to the bedroom, put a chair underneath the door and sat on the bed. Then I heard a loud knock saying it was the police. I thought the neighbors that saw me run past must have called them.

After talking with them, I learned that he had called the police, thinking he could talk his way out of what had happened.

But he was arrested with the text I sent and the imprint of my face (makeup) on the bed with blood on it. There was no denying what had transpired. He said I was going for a gun and he was trying to protect me from hurting myself. He later changed his story to I had attacked him (with the scratches on his arms) and he was defending himself. He was arrested for assault in the second degree and the story aired on the news because he was a police officer. That day I had so many people reach out to me. No longer could I be silent about what happened. He was released on bail the next day with an automatic protection order in place. He was not to stay at the house. So he lived in our camper.

I stayed with him there for one hellish week and I want to emphasize how common this is. I went back because I wanted to believe we could get beyond the assault. I went back because he was my husband and I loved him. I went back because I did not want him to lose his job. I went back because I hoped that it would be the wake-up call he needed in order to change. After meeting with his lawyer I even tried to take a letter to the court lifting the order of protection saying that I must have passed out from screaming too hard (because that is a thing, right?).

But he was more worried about losing his job than what happened to me.

He agreed to go to counseling with me if it would be with his old counselor. We went and that was the day I chose to leave. I had written a letter of everything I could think of that led up to that point. I chose to read it to the counselor so I could get everything out without letting too much emotion rule the conversation. When I got done he looked at his counselor and said, "see what I have to put up with?" and she looked over at me and said "do you think if you would have responded differently he would have done what he did to you?" In that very instant, there was clarity, there was anger, there was a flood of all the emotions I had wanted to feel but had minimized. I left that day knowing I was done, that I no longer was going to be a victim to this man's lies, deceit, manipulation, narcissism, violence and evil. It was the first time I felt like I was in control of my future.

My mother came back with me to help me move. She brought life back to me. She wrote several Bible verses throughout the apartment to flood my mind with truth because there had been so many lies he told me about myself. I was having nightmares, panic attacks and crying.

I called a friend who was a defense attorney and asked him about getting a family lawyer. He gave me a name and also told me that my husband's first wife, Staci, was a friend of his and she wanted to talk with me if I wanted. She was his son's mother, the one with the book of investigations against him, so I texted her. What transpired during our text conversation was truly an act of divine intervention. We connected on a level that no one else could understand. We decided to meet and I cannot tell you what a blessing that meeting was. Staci and I talked about her relationship with him, and we both started to feel heard, seen, understood and not alone. She made me feel like I was sane while he tried to convince me that I was the "crazy" one.

I knew in order to proceed forward I needed to get help.

I met with a trauma therapist who suggested I do EMDR (Eye Movement Desensitization Reprocessing) therapy. I went to eight sessions and it helped by giving me the tools to confront the pain and nightmares, and to walk gently in the present moment.

During that time, I also remembered I had a brochure that the police officer gave me the night he arrested my ex. It was for a women's crisis center. I did not know what services they could offer, but I needed help financially and that was the initial reason I went there. When I started talking with the victim's advocate lawyer, she made me feel so comfortable. She heard me, completely understood where I was coming from and suggested I speak to one of the counselors there. I went weekly and started to trust myself again and heal the scars and wounds of my crushed self-esteem. I cannot express how grateful I am for this crisis center; therefore, I choose to give back a portion of our profits at SPEAK Cosmetics to this center, along with another local crisis center.

I also gathered enough courage to meet with the special prosecutor who was assigned to my case against my ex. For months we met and Staci even met with us. Our world was about putting this man in jail and not letting him destroy another life physically and emotionally. Although there was an order of protection in place for two years, there was a constant fear that he might break it. In the end the special prosecutor chose to offer a plea deal that involved him taking an eight-week course in domestic abuse as well as giving up his peace officer's license (which meant he would not be able to be a police officer anywhere). I did not want to offer a plea deal, but he told me it was the "county" against him and not me personally. I could have filed a civil suit but chose not to. I am at least thankful that he is no longer a police officer and there is not that "credibility" to his name. However, even though he agreed to the plea deal, he never went to the anger management workshop. I believe to this day he talks himself into believing what happened was not his fault.

***I have healed from the damage he has done.
For me my Faith proved to be the most influential.***

When I could replace the lies that he told me with Scripture, that was the first step to changing my thought process. I flooded my mind, thoughts, audio books and reading with words of truth from the Bible. I also learned how to reach out to friends for help. That was such a hard step for me but I found that I had a community of women surrounding me with open arms and I am most proud of the work I chose to do to promote my healing.

If you do not have the community of support from friends or family, that is where a crisis center will step in. They will be your friends and family, they will offer aid when you don't know where to start. They are incredibly skilled at knowing exactly how to help you create a safety plan and when you are ready to leave, they will help you put steps in place so you can put one foot in front of the other.

Also, don't be like the people that saw me outside my apartment that night. If you feel something isn't right with a neighbor, acquaintance, friend or family member, make sure they are all right. Ask if they need help. Don't be a bystander.

I refuse to allow myself to stay in a victim mindset. I have forgiven this man and I don't hold onto what he did to me. But it did light a fire under me to help others, to be a voice to the voiceless, to offer support and advocacy to so many hurting in silence. Since my story aired publicly on the news, I was given a platform that did not allow me to stay silent and I am so grateful for that. At the time, I did not know it would be a blessing but now it allows me to be here, to be in this space to SPEAK for you.

I don't know you, but I know how hurt and confused you may be feeling. I know the tightness in your chest. I know you wake up not knowing what "face" your partner will put on that day. I know the struggle of wondering how you can word everything to lessen the chance of there being an argument and what violence it might cause.

I'm here to tell you that love doesn't hurt. And love shouldn't involve you hurting yourself physically either. I know he or she may tell you they don't know how they would live without you and frankly you may feel you may not be able to survive without them either. You WILL, YOU CAN and not only survive but my beautiful friend, you will thrive. You are stronger than you could ever imagine and the shell who you once were will become filled with confidence, perseverance and resilience. You will heal and you will love again.

My story has a happy ending. I am now married to a loving, incredible, kindhearted man and together we have two beautiful baby boys and a wonderful stepson. I am gentle with myself, giving myself grace for the hard days, loving myself on the even more difficult days and thankful for every moment of every day.

So please listen to that uncomfortable feeling, don't push it down— let it fuel you to take action. There is a whole world waiting for you to live in it and not be silenced in the shadows.

I love you and I have such extraordinary hope for you.

You are being presented with a choice:
evolve or remain. If you choose to remain
unchanged, you will be presented with the
same challenges, the same routine, the same
storms, the same situations, until you
learn from them, until you love yourself
to say "no more", until you choose change.
If you choose to evolve, you will connect
with the strength within you, you will
explore what lies outside the comfort
zone, you will awaken to love,
you will become, you will be.
You have everything you need.
Choose to evolve.
Choose love.

~ Creig Crippen

Renee Courier Aumock from Michigan
Photographed by Alisa Divine

From Pain to Purpose

Trauma doesn't just go away. There's no magic button, magic day or magic age when it all disappears and you're free. There's no just "getting over it." Don't we wish it was that easy? If you've experienced trauma, especially in childhood, you know it's definitely not as easy as "getting over it." It consumes us. It seeps into every pore. It puts us into survival mode. Our thoughts, our feelings, and our actions toward ourselves and toward others ALL are affected by our trauma, sometimes for the rest of our lives. Trauma rewires the brain. That doesn't mean we can't heal from and cope with our trauma as adults, but at times, it can be a daily battle. Emotions can be GIANTS. There's no forgetting. There's only coping.

I was born to teenage parents. Like other teens, they were kids who were still growing and maturing. They were young and raised their children with the skills they had at the time. I am so thankful to my parents for doing the best they could at such a young age. I can't imagine how it felt to be responsible for children at that time in their lives. Thankfully, they had a great support system in both of their families. Unfortunately, back then, my grandparents' church shunned my family because I was born to unwed parents. The church wouldn't even baptize me because I was born from that sin. My father had a tough childhood growing up with 10 siblings in a strict Catholic family. My grandpa thought it was okay to use physical force as regular parenting and discipline (because that is how he was raised). That upbringing negatively affected my dad and influenced how he parented. He never hit us but I do remember feeling fear when he got angry. Since my dad didn't know how to heal his childhood pain, he turned to substances to numb it.

I wonder how different our lives would have been if it had been easier to recognize abuse then and ask for help to heal from it without judgment. As I got older, I earned the title of 'the fixer" as I tried to find the right words to make things better even though it never seemed to work. I hated when my dad was upset and would do whatever I could to change the situation. My role often left me questioning my own self-worth as I internalized his anger to be my fault. I wanted nothing more than to win his approval and make everything okay. If you have had any type of trauma or neglect in childhood (even if you think it was small), I encourage you to learn about how it affects you and seek resources to heal from it. Breaking the cycle of generational trauma is so important for everyone in this story.

Later, I attracted what I knew and what love I thought I deserved. At 16, the same age as my daughter now, I fell in love with a "bad boy." I used the relationship skills I learned as "the fixer" with my new boyfriend. I worked hard for acceptance — I wanted to make him happy, so he would not cheat on me, hurt me or break my heart. I so badly hoped I could help my broken boyfriend, the young man who shared early childhood experiences of addiction, abuse and a lack of love. On our good days he opened his heart to me and I felt such compassion for this kindred spirit. But on most days he declared no one else would tolerate or love me. And I believed him, allowing him to treat me poorly. He cheated, lied, threatened, kicked, pushed and beat me. He mastered the art of "I'm sorry, but you just make me so mad sometimes!"

> *Many nights the police were called to my rescue.*
> *I suspect they looked at me as the stereotypical,*
> *undeserving lost cause like so many others they*
> *served on any given shift on any given night.*

He was forced to leave but he always came back. He was an addict. I naively believed if I could love him enough, he would seek help — he would recover and he would love me. Sure, he got sober a few times, but in the end he got worse. No one told me I did not have to live that way. No one discussed dating violence or domestic violence. I wonder, if the police officers had talked to me about what was going on, would I have left sooner? If they would have given me local resources to help, would I have used them? I also wonder, if my ex had been mandated therapy sessions during one of his many times in jail or prison, would he have had the chance to heal? Being incarcerated for an addiction doesn't cure the addiction and it certainly doesn't reveal and heal the hurt underneath. The definition of insanity is continuing to do the same things while expecting or hoping for different results.

It was not until I was in my early 20s that I mustered the strength to kick him out permanently — or so I thought. I had met another man. I felt like it was too good to be true, someone so kind, loving and tolerant. He was sooooo nice! I did not think I deserved that attention and type of love. It was not in my wheelhouse of experience. I felt unworthy of him, so ultimately I played the self-defeating role. Part of it was fear of rejection and part of it was self-preservation — I bailed and returned to the chaos because it was familiar.

> *I can't help but wonder what could have happened*
> *if I had gotten the help I needed to heal from the abuse*
> *way back then, instead of allowing it to continue*
> *for years to come.*

I jumped in and out of my abusive relationship and found myself unwed and pregnant with my abuser's child at the age of 26. Like many mothers, I hoped this baby would fix us and persuade the father to be better. He got sober and was on good behavior for a few months but ended up moving out for our safety. He was able to visit with his daughter at my house when I was present and he was sober. These visits were inconsistent. One night when my daughter was a toddler, we came home to find him in our house intoxicated and passed out naked on the toilet. My daughter, filled with fear and questions, thought he was dead. I lied and told her he was just tired and not feeling well. I asked her to go to her room and shut the door to play for a while.
Always the fixer.

Another night while my daughter was visiting my parents he beat me worse than ever before, leaving me with black and blue bruises from my neck to my feet. I thought I was going to die that night. It was different from the other times because that time if I died, I would be leaving my little girl behind. There were many other incidents like these. I hated that my daughter had to live like that. She deserved so much more. My worst fear was that something would happen to me and my daughter would not have me to protect her. I thought to myself, "What am I doing?" It was very messy but we parted ways — again.

Unfortunately, when my daughter was in preschool, my ex decided to seek out visitation through the Friend of the Court (FOC). I ended up taking him back in fear of what could happen to her if I wasn't around to protect her. I did not trust the safety of court ordered visitations with him.

I could not afford a lawyer as a single mom and I was desperate to keep her safe. Thank God I received free advice to request random drug tests. They assured me this would work based on their professional experience. I called the FOC office and begged them not to require me to meet with my ex face to face. I told them I was afraid for mine and my daughter's safety. They didn't seem to care and told me if I didn't show up I would be in contempt of court.

> *I didn't have a choice.*
> *No matter how frightened I was,*
> *I had to protect my daughter*
> *and do it in front of my abuser.*

Despite the numerous facts and proof I presented, the mediator still ruled on his behalf. Too often, agencies that protect children believe that because a parent is biological, they can be trusted to keep their children safe without supervision (we will get back to this shortly). I was thankful I knew the magic words – "I am requesting random drug tests" and they had to accommodate this due to his prior drug arrests.

Of course my ex was livid with me. I knew I would be paying the price for that one. But at least I saved my daughter for the moment. I wonder what would have happened if I hadn't learned those magic words from someone who chose to help me. Not everyone has access to the same resources. I wonder what happens to all the other kids who are forced to see a toxic parent simply because they are biological.

After that meeting I was filled with anxiety and fear of what was to come. I received phone calls from my ex threatening to kill me. I didn't know what to do. I called the police for help. I told them I had a voicemail in my ex's voice, recorded from his phone number threatening to kill me. They told me it was hearsay and they couldn't help me. WHAT? That was not hearsay, it was a fact WITH proof. My thoughts raced. Are they not obligated to protect me and my daughter? With no help from the authorities, in fear of our lives, my daughter and I stayed with my parents for a few weeks until my ex calmed down.

My hope for the future is that agencies charged with protecting children realize not all biological parents should have rights. Not only is it wrong, it is putting children in tragic situations resulting in horrible consequences. I wonder what would happen if those agencies would realize that not all biological parents deserve rights. Would our community have more healthy members? Would there be less crime? Would we have fewer addicts and fewer people overdosing as they try to numb the pain? I have to answer this so it isn't missed – YES to all of them!

Go back to the quote that opened this story. Trauma affects people, especially trauma experienced in childhood. If we allow addicted, traumatized, abused biological parents to continue the generational cycle with their children, this toxic cycle will never end. Let's wake up, turn the system upside down and PROTECT our babies. This was not the only time I fought for my daughter's safety. I eventually ended up signing off financially so my ex wouldn't be responsible for child support, which I never got anyway. There was a silent agreement between my ex and me — I could keep my daughter safe and he could keep his money for partying. I wonder what our lives could have been if the system protected me and my daughter while still allowing me to receive child support.

I didn't understand why they fought harder for an addict with a long criminal record than a single mom trying to do her best working and going to college.

Clearly, my daughter saved my life. I felt pure love for the first time from the moment I knew I was pregnant. But I was scared. I was unemployed. I was uneducated, broken and alone. My first priority was to provide for my little girl. Obviously I wanted her basic needs to be met, but I also wanted to provide her with experiences and opportunities I had missed. It wasn't until I was laid off from my well-paid position at a local factory more than one year before my daughter was born that I understood the importance of post secondary education. Although my high school diploma was enough earlier, I struggled to find viable work as post-secondary training became more of a requirement for many of the positions I sought. I saw a commercial for a medical billing and coding course which I could complete in one year with a guaranteed job. I was afraid to go to a university. I was afraid of failing. However, I surprised myself with how well I did in college that first year. I am thankful for the help of my parents, sibling and family. They supported my endeavor and helped parent my daughter while I attended class part time and studied.

My college advisor saw something in me that I did not see in myself.

Somehow she knew I would love the opportunity to help others. I thought she had to be wrong. How in the world could I help others when I felt I could barely help myself? After I was beaten down emotionally and physically for so long I did not believe I had anything to give. But my advisor worked with the local community foundation and soon I was employed there through a work-study position with the university.

That was a lifesaver financially because I quickly learned that our systems trap people in poverty. I was on state assistance for food and medical insurance for the first time in my life. For me it was only to help care for my daughter during her earliest years while I was working diligently at becoming self-sufficient once again. Even so, I was lumped into the group of people who "live off welfare." I was appalled by the quality of treatment I received from Medicaid-approved healthcare systems. I also learned that if I gained income, my benefits could get taken from me. Since my work-study was considered government money, it didn't count as income and it didn't affect my assistance. That has been a valuable piece of information for many who I've crossed paths with, especially during my speaking engagements at the local Women's Center and YWCA. We need to share more nuggets of helpful information to those who need it. That opportunity gave me wonderful experience, an education of business and a nonprofit, and helped me build my professional network — which later led to working with many agencies and making a difference. Turning my pain into purpose became my focus.

I eventually earned my intended certificate of medical billing and coding. It gave me confidence, something I had been seeking my entire life. For once I was proud and had a skill set to move me toward two associate degrees, a bachelor's degree and a master's. I proudly claim I came from a first generation high school graduate to a master's degree graduate in strategic management. The irony of a degree in strategic management still makes me chuckle!

My hope here is that more businesses that require further education would also assist their staff with funding. Especially single parents. Everyone in a community has a moral responsibility to lift others up instead of tear them down. I also wonder what would happen if more of our community leaders were held to higher standards and accountable for how they treated staff. These leaders could be supporting a victim to stay in their unhealthy home relationship because they also are in an unhealthy work environment.

I wonder what would happen if leaders and their staff were trained to recognize the signs of abuse and what to do when spotted.

One of my most significant personal changes occurred when my daughter was 8 months old. During our first Father's Day alone, I chose to attend a church service near my parents' house. God must work in mysterious ways as the shunned baby of unwed parents chose to attend church as a single mother. Maybe it was the miracle of my own daughter. I held her the entire service. I stood as the music played while I was swaying, crying and hugging my perfect little girl. I had never heard church/worship music like that before. My heart was touched that day, and I was forever changed.

A member of the congregation noticed that I had been crying and asked if I needed to chat after service. I said yes. I cannot even remember the details of the conversation, but I remember how I felt — accepted. I could not wait to go back. I wonder now if the church would have loved and welcomed my parents when I was young like God teaches, maybe my family's lives would have been different? The church today is often still guilty of judging and shunning certain people. What they don't realize is that loving people is more important than whose beliefs are right or wrong. Welcoming someone has much more power than preaching how wrong their ways are. Thankfully, that time, God gave me hope, joy and the strength to make it through each week. I realized I was not raising my daughter alone. She had a Father in the Lord. We became very involved in the church, built a support system and learned more about God and a wonderful new way of living. I felt God directing me and giving me strength and confidence to do things I never would have done before.

> *Getting to my new normal has not been easy.*
> *I stumbled and ran into many roadblocks,*
> *some of my own creation and others*
> *from the system as I see it.*

Victims of trauma develop defense mechanisms, some bad and unhealthy habits. Sometimes it is difficult to recognize we are operating out of anxiety and fear. I learned to follow the Lord's guidance. He put me in places where I could begin to save lives. One specific example was my collaboration with the FOC in a program I created, The Great Lakes Bay College and Career Resource Center. This program provided resources and support to help people of all ages attain the necessary education to find meaningful and gainful employment. We also provided assistance to adults needing positive changes to ensure they could care for themselves and their families. I used my personal experience to connect with people and used my professional experiences and education to help them build a brighter future.

As a result of this program, I gained the respect and trust of the FOC director. Ten years after my first experience, I had a conversation with the director and she was accommodating of my requests to stop enabling within the system. I told her my story and she had no idea. She was genuinely remorseful of the negative impact her office had on the safety of me and my little girl. I was able to educate and be part of the changes they implemented for others to come including questioning clients on abuse and not requiring them to meet face to face with their abuser. Through my participation in this book, I also discovered Alisa was positively affected through the changes. Romans 8:28 deeply impacted me when I read it for the first time: "And we know that in all things God works for the good of those who love him, who have been called to his purpose." I learned that God could turn all the pain I went through into a purpose if I let it. It felt like a divine intervention to work with the FOC. I wonder what would happen if we all found a way to turn our pain into a purpose? I also wonder what would happen if more agencies were willing to hear from those they serve and make positive changes accordingly?

When I continued to share my story with others, I could see the lightbulb illuminate as they realized if I could overcome my struggles, so could they. I continued speaking at the Women's Center, the Great Lakes Bay Region YWCA, and the Good Samaritan Rescue Mission. I spoke to students at local high schools, especially connecting with those attending the alternative schools as I was able to relate to difficult childhoods, abusive relationships, single motherhood, the uneducated, the unemployed and the marginalized members of society. I honestly do not believe I could have reached so many without living the pain myself.

Even though my ex wasn't a part of my life any longer,
I realized it was important for me to learn to forgive
and even pray for him.

This helped me to live out my purpose instead of living in the pain he caused. I understand his demons are huge. But today they are his demons, not mine. I learned some valuable lessons along the way. First, you cannot fix him. He will only take you down with him. Second, pay attention to the elements of a healthy relationship. Recognize if you are acting out or feeling hurt, it could be from a past trauma. You must do the work to heal from within before you date. Hurt people attract other hurt people. Third, break a generational chain of dysfunctional behavior — addiction, abuse, poverty. Pass a healthy baton to the ones who follow. Lastly, find your support system before you leave and hang onto them. Professional counselling, support groups, online resources, social media pages and groups, religious organizations are out there. I think back at how my path to a healthy life may have been shorter.

In closing, my journey is similar to many. I feel like my story, once filled with desperation, anger, embarrassment and PAIN, is now filled with healing, empathy, hope and PURPOSE. I have allowed God to funnel my story to those I can encourage. I am a work in progress. I continue, with the help of others, to recognize the habits and mindsets that occasionally hold me back. I can only hope my daughter has learned from me, not only the importance — but also, the strength and courage it takes to ask for help. I continue to pray that the Lord watches over my daughter, keeps her safe and shows her a true Father's love. She is an amazing young lady and I am incredibly proud of her. I know God has big plans for her. I will forever be grateful to her for saving me.

The Bible says that we will overcome by the word of our testimony. I believe this is true because it happened to me. I hear your voices filled with fear and desperation. I believe in the hope that we all can overcome.

Her smile hid things, the way that family photos
sometimes cover fist holes in a wall.

~ John Mark Green

Brandi Smith from Arkansas
Photographed by Monica Westbrook

Built on Lies

I met him at a casino but looking back, that night was anything but lucky.

He was not someone I would have ever been interested in dating — he had dreads which I don't prefer, he smoked, he was shorter and heavier than what I usually am attracted to — but we sat there for three hours beside each other just talking and laughing and having a good time playing the slot machines. We exchanged numbers. Because we were long distance I assumed it would go nowhere. But soon after we were talking every night and for some reason I was like a schoolgirl with a huge crush. I couldn't wait for him to call or send a text. He was so intrigued with me, my kids, my family, my life. He wanted to know everything about me. He showered me with compliments and made me feel like he cared. Before I knew it, he was traveling to see me.

He would come down every Saturday and we would go out to eat. He would always get a room in town and we would continue talking there. Nothing got sexual at first. After about a month things got serious and he started coming and staying all weekend, but still at a hotel. And finally about four months in, I let my guard down and introduced him to my kids. He fed me this poor pitiful story about how he grew up with no dad, his mom was on drugs and there were times that he and his siblings had to eat out of a dumpster. So I felt sorry for him.

He would give me money if I needed it. He always put us first and made me happy. He acted so genuine and gave up a 25-year job and his whole life in west Memphis. He cut his dreads, stopped smoking for me and changed his wardrobe.

He started staying at my house with us on the weekends. Then the relationship moved very fast.

About nine months after we started talking, he moved in. I felt so comfortable with him that looking back I know now it was all built on lies and narcissistic behavior. He worked out a way with his boss to draw unemployment, cleaned the house and paid bills. Once his unemployment ran out, he got two jobs.

And for a year, he treated me like a princess.

He complimented me daily and always told me he was so lucky to have me and the kids as his new family. We began planning a wedding. I was so excited because I had never been married before and I finally found the love of my life.

The wedding was everything I expected because I didn't expect a lot. The honeymoon was a cruise and it was great. Things were fine between us until four months into our marriage. It started to unravel and he became very jealous and controlling. He wanted to know who was calling or texting me or who was on Facebook. He somehow was able to receive my texts and phone calls and turned on the "find my phone" feature on his phone so he always knew where I was. He questioned my every move and then he would call me a liar.

Things got worse when he started working two jobs. He wanted to know why I stayed later than my 12-hour shifts, although I explained that working as the team manager at an urgent care meant I couldn't leave until the last patient did. When he came to the urgent care to have his blood pressure monitored, he didn't like that there were so many male patients.

His relationship with my children also changed. He and my daughter never really got close. I assumed it was because they both were shy. They didn't talk much. I guess I wasn't surprised when she moved out on her own shortly after we got married. She was 20 years old.

But my son was only 9 years old. When he first moved in he took Tanner to school and picked him up. I thought that my son had finally found a father figure. He had someone to play video games with and basketball. He also took him to the pool at the apartment park. But after my daughter moved out, my son started acting like he didn't want to be around him anymore. When I voiced my unhappiness to him, that's when the threats and abuse began. He told me if I ever tried to leave him he would slit my son's throat, then mine, then he would kill himself. The abuse raged on — beatings, choking, holding knives to my neck. Forced bedroom activity and anal rape. All the while he reminded me that if I told anyone he would get to one of my kids and kill them.

I was devastated, confused, felt betrayed and most of all terrified because there was no doubt that this man was going to kill me or one of my kids. He changed so quickly and told me that he needed mental help because he couldn't sleep, eat or work without thinking that I was out cheating. However, I never gave him a reason to think that. He even showed me a paper where he wrote the addresses of my daughter's home, school and work and my son's school ready to put them in his gps and get to one of my kids if I told anyone or tried to leave him. There was no way I was going to take that chance. I had to figure out what to do myself quickly because he was unstable.

There was constant tension in our house and our relationship was deteriorating.

My son and I came home one day and he was in one of his moods where he accused me of being out with some guy. I could tell he had been drinking because he was yelling and acting crazy in front of Tanner. So I walked into the back room away from my son because I could see he was getting worried. My ex followed me and tried to trap me in the bathroom. I kept trying to come out and he kept pushing me back in. We were in the doorway when Tanner walked in right as he pushed me into the wall and broke the towel hanger. I tried to run out. I made it to the doorway in between my room and the dining room when he caught me. I could see directly into the kitchen as I was trying to fight my way through the doorway.

Tanner looked at us with pure terror on his little face. I kept pleading with my ex to let me go. And he said we would all die if I tried to leave him. By that time Tanner reached the kitchen drawer and pulled out a knife and had it pointed toward him. He slowly

64

started walking towards us. My ex would not let me go. He kept yelling at Tanner, daring him to come and stab him, because without his mom, he was dead anyways. Tanner was in a fog but he kept walking toward us. I shouted at Tanner to "look at momma" but he wouldn't. If I got his attention I thought I could distract him.

Tanner had this horrible look of fear and anger. He got closer and my ex got louder, saying, "Do it! Do it! Stab me right here!"

Somehow I found the strength to elbow him in the stomach, push him out of the way and pull Tanner into the room with me. As I did, the knife fell. I locked the door to my bedroom. But he had my phone. My ex got to the door, unlocked it and burst in with the knife in his hand. In front of Tanner and me he slit his wrist. He then walked out of the room and shut the door.

I felt no pity for him. I didn't even care.

Tanner and I sat there for a few hours. Tanner fell asleep. He came back in with paper towels wrapped around his wrist. That time he had a box cutter in his hand. He looked right at me and said if I dared to tell anyone or tried to leave, it would only take him a second to slit Tanner's throat. I knew he would do it. I was stuck. He had threatened to slit Tanner's throat before, then mine, then his and I knew he would do it. Tanner and I stayed in the house for two days after that, unable to leave. I told Tanner that he accidentally took the wrong medicine with some alcohol he was drinking and it made him act crazy. I didn't want Tanner to tell anyone before I could do something myself.

His way of apologizing for that event was coming home the next day with a huge tattoo on his back shoulder of a heart with the names "Tan, Tay, and Bran" with a dagger through it and a drip of blood coming out of it. He said his heart bleeds for us. And just like the tattoo was permanent, the message was that our family was permanent too.

I knew I had to get out. I knew I had to take control. There was no doubt in my mind that he was going to kill me. And I didn't know how to get away but I knew I had to do it. I planned to make my move after my daughter's 21st birthday party. I didn't want to ruin Taylor's day since her dad and stepmom were planning a party for her. I have a wonderful relationship with my children's father and stepmother. So we were invited to their house for the party to watch Taylor receive her dream car from her father. I wasn't going to miss that.

My ex was not going to let me go by myself. On the way there he poured six straight shots of gin into a venti-size Starbucks cup and he drank the whole thing. He was jealous of the relationship between my father's children and me. And he was not happy that we were going there. When we arrived I asked him not to mess up Taylor's party. But it was at Taylor's birthday party that he lost it. He snapped and almost killed me.

He drank and played cards for a couple hours. But he would come over and whisper to me, "Wait till we get home, I'm going to fuck you up. I see you flirting with everyone." This went on throughout the day and then at one point, he grabbed the back of my neck and that's when my kids' dad and my daughter ran over. My kids' dad grabbed him and said, "You're not going to put your hands on the mother of my children. As a matter of fact, you need to leave." And he escorted him out of the driveway to the street where all the cars were parked. They were arguing and he said, "Let's go, Brandi." But I told him I was not going with him.

He said he needed his phone so my son went inside and brought it to me. I went to give it to him. There was a lot going on around us. It was loud. There were people in the street, in the driveway, and he was sitting in the driver's seat of the car with the door open. With all the noise I didn't hear that he started the car. I walked around to his open door to hand him his phone and that's when he reached up, grabbed me by the neck of my shirt and floored the car.

I was dragged under the car about 500 feet. I could feel my skin being scraped off my feet, legs and backside.

I saw my feet dangling by the back tires and I knew if he let go of me, I'd be run over. My shoes flew off. I looked up and saw my 21-year-old daughter running after the car with panic in her eyes.

I knew that if her face was the last face I saw before I died, I would be okay. He continued driving until I couldn't see anymore. He came to a stop, grabbed me and pulled me into the passenger seat and took off. He started beating me and said we were both going to die. I managed to put my seatbelt on, put my head down and closed my eyes.

I prayed to God to take care of my kids.

I could feel the car going faster. And making sharp turns. He floored it again and BAM — we hit a tree on my side. He came around to my side but the tree trapped me. So he pulled me out from his side of the car. I was barefoot and there was broken glass all over the ground. He threw me down on the concrete, got on top of me and started banging my head on the concrete several times. Then he stood up and with his boots on, kicked me in the head, then my face, then my neck. He knocked all of my teeth out.

That's when I heard the sirens. He realized he wasn't going to get to kill me. So he got on top of me in an attempt to dismember my face. He tried ripping my mouth open. He bit and broke my thumb. He bit a chunk out of my hand. Then he bit a chunk out of my face. As they were pulling him off me, he grabbed my eye and tried to pull it out. He twisted it, ripping the muscles.

The police arrested him on the spot for attempted aggravated kidnapping. The judge didn't set bail because as they put me on the gurney he told the police officers that when he made bail, he was coming to kill me and the kids. It took two years for the trial but he finally was sentenced to 18 years for 1st degree attempted murder and attempted kidnapping. I found out that everything I thought I knew about him was a lie. He was narcissistic. The past he told me about was all a lie. The truth came out. He had prior violence charges that were dropped.

Once he was arrested, my children and I began our own nightmare. It is not easy to deal with the aftermath from domestic violence. I've worried about my kids throughout this whole ordeal. The things that they had seen. And heard. And had to deal with it first hand.

As I was in my recovery process, my son started acting out. I knew there was going to be some sort of impact from what he heard and saw. He was angry. He was rude to my parents. Not as much to me but to everyone else. He was not the son I raised. He would run down the road, away from my parents' house when they watched him. He was destructive, unruly and had a foul mouth. I didn't know what to do to control his behavior. He even tried to hurt himself. His little body was so full of anger and hatred. I had no choice but to put him into Pinnacle Point, a behavioral healthcare for children and teens.

While at the facility, he continued with cries for help. He fought, spit at others, cursed. I felt broken. My son wasn't with me, he was there for five months. I fell into a dark depression.

Then he started to do what the counselors suggested. He participated in therapy and their programs and started doing his class work. At one of our family sessions when he was 10 years old, he stood up and said, "Mom, you know how you go around and tell your story, (he was referring to me speaking about my abuse to different audiences), well here is mine." Then he read from four sheets of paper about how my ex physically abused him as well as hit him, shoved him, called him names like "punk" and "momma's little bitch boy." And he told my son that if he ever "told on him," he would slit my throat and it would be Tanner's fault. So after I was almost killed, Tanner went through all the emotions of guilt, anger, sadness and confusion. Bless his heart. My son was living with the guilt that I almost died because he said nothing.

And I couldn't handle it. I was traumatized all over again. I was at a loss and wondering how it could have happened and I never knew about it.

I blamed myself. And I wanted my ex dead.
I wanted him to pay for what he did to my son.

I also wanted him to pay for what he did to my daughter, who will never get the image out of her mind of her mother being dragged under a car. She had to be put on medication. She had nightmares, insomnia, went through depression and cried buckets of tears. She also went through her own stage of guilt, thinking maybe if she wouldn't have moved out of the house her mom and her brother would have never been abused. Somehow she felt she could have protected us. And she had guilt over not telling me that she didn't care for my ex because she knew that I never would have been with someone that my kids didn't approve of.

My daughter ran after the car as I was dragged under it until she couldn't see me anymore. She fell to her knees, unable to catch her breath because she thought she would never see me again. Her mom, her best friend. How was I going to help her through that? I worried so much about my kids and yet I think they were stronger than me. They helped me get through it. My son told me he was going to be okay. He just wanted me to be okay. Without my kids — I wouldn't have been able to make it through the rough journey and heal.

The journey back from the abuse has been a rough five years.

I have had operations on my mouth, my teeth, and my thumb. I have had several surgeries on my face where he bit the chunk out and I have had several surgeries on my bad eye and then one on my good eye.

For the first eight months my right eye had to stay closed because I had horrible double vision. When he grabbed my eye he did so much damage. My eye was twisted and moved to the point that opening it was impossible. Then I had a huge patch of fatty skin directly under my eye where he bit a chunk out of my face. The doctors had to do emergency surgery that night and did a skin graft from my chest. Needless to say, I was definitely stared at and was very self conscious. The eye injury affected my driving and my job. I was in the medical field so going back to work was a struggle because I gave injections, drew blood and did x-rays. I basically had to learn to live with one eye for eight months while the world around me stared at me like I was a monster. That was hard for me but it was even harder on my kids to see and witness others constantly stare and whisper when we would go places.

Wearing a mask also has been a struggle for me because it reminds me of when my abuser put his hand over my mouth when he forced me to have sex. I don't go out in public as much as I used to because of my anxiety. Driving in a car also gives me anxiety. I am okay though and I am getting through everything one day at a time.

As far as my mental health goes, I have PTSD. I have seen my therapist every one to two weeks for more than three years now. I have a mild traumatic brain injury, anxiety, nightmares, insomnia and triggers. I also developed trauma induced narcolepsy. There was enough head trauma that I'm no longer quick and on the spot as I used to be. Sometimes I get things confused. And sometimes I forget what I am talking about. I may get my words mixed up or forget my own phone number.

In order to continue my recovery, I have spoken at many events and colleges to tell my story. I'm an advocate for domestic abuse and sexual abuse. My daughter has been to each of my speaking engagements. She cried buckets of tears alongside me. Our relationship could not be stronger.

I have never talked about what happened to my son at any of my speaking events or to be honest anywhere. A lot of my family doesn't even know. This is the first place I have actually spoken about it and I did talk to Tanner about it first because it is his story. But I am his mother, his protector and with his permission and some things kept private, this is my way of making sure that what my ex did to my son does not go unnoticed. It also lets whoever reads my story know that not only did that sorry piece of shit put his hands on women but on an innocent child.

Surprisingly, my story received national attention.
I was on the daytime TV show, The Doctors,
in 2016 and 2017 after TV news coverage
in Tennessee and Arkansas.

The experience was so empowering because I knew how big the audience was. The doctors were absolutely amazing, so real, involved and concerned. Because of the show, I had an amazing group of doctors do several surgeries on my eye and face at no charge. They accomplished fixing my double vision when looking straight ahead. I still have it looking up or down and I can't see looking to my right. I have to turn my whole head but omg it's 90 percent better than what it was. One of my biggest eye surgeries was even on camera! The doctors also got rid of almost all of my fatty pocket.

> *I'm left with a pretty good scar but it tells my story*
> *so I have grown to be okay with it.*

There also was a spine doctor from the show who gave me $5,000 to help towards my medical bills. I was overwhelmed with gratitude. The Women's Own Worth Foundation helped me get my teeth fixed at Little Rock Family Dental. They were such wonderful people and there was no charge to me at all. I felt so blessed. They helped me get my smile back.

However, flying back and forth to LA to *The Doctors Show* and having surgeries had a serious effect on my son. That was when he started acting out for my parents and it was necessary to send him to Pinnacle Point. My parents have been there to take care of me and my kids whenever we needed them. My mom took care of me the first month after the attack. She became another source of strength. She took me to every doctor appointment for the first two years and still goes with me now whenever allowed. My parents only went to one of my speaking events and it was hard on them to hear my story, especially my dad. I am okay with that. I've had an amazing support system of family and friends, but it was my kids that helped get me through everything. They have been my biggest supporters.

Both of them often tell me, "Mom, you're the strongest person I know." But to me, they are the strongest people I know. And they have been my rock.

I haven't let that horrible marriage shut my life down. I have volunteered at our local women's shelter. My goal is to start a nonprofit one day to help men and women recover after they have been in a domestic violence or sexual violence situation. Because it's not easy even after it's over.

I still go through struggles. I have fallen and been at my lowest so many times but I keep picking myself up. I have to do it for myself but also because my kids have faith in me and I refuse to let them down. Certainly I am a different person after all of this but hell, who wouldn't be? I am now more educated on the red flags and I'm more observant. I feel like I'm more of a hardass, not so naive to sad sob stories. I think about myself more these days and I definitely don't worry about what others think. I have to put my needs first. I had to stop saying yes to everyone else before putting my own needs first, thinking that it was a selfless act. The truth is it's exhausting and I'm good to no one if I'm emotionally, mentally, and physically burned out.

Clearly, he did not get the best of me. Yes, I've cried a lot. Yes, I've wanted to give up. I've asked why I didn't see the signs. I've asked how I could've been so stupid. But no more of that. I have stopped blaming myself and realized that none of us deserved any of his abusive behaviors. God was with me that day. And I'm here for a reason. One is for my kids. And the second is to help others who have been through abuse.

We have to speak up and speak out. We have to convince others that there is no excuse for abuse.

My final thought...

She has been broken.
She has been knocked down.
She has been defeated.
She has felt the pain that most couldn't handle.

She looks fear in the face.
Day after day, year after year.
But yet, she never runs,
She never hides.
And she always finds a way to get back up.

She is unbreakable.
She's a warrior and a survivor .
SHE IS YOU!

*"Women don't need to find a voice,
they have a voice,
and they need to feel empowered to use it,
and people need to be encouraged to listen."*

~ Meghan Markle

Christina Williams from Pennsylvania

Photographed by Hannah Trott

The Great Escape

I sat down in the beat up brown leather recliner chair across from my counselor's desk. Her desk was filled with tons of paperwork, pictures of her significant other, and her water bottle. She was sitting in her less comfortable desk chair while filling out information on her computer. I was looking around and at the same time checking out the art hanging on the walls. They looked like the kind you would find in the picture frame or housewares section of TJ Maxx or Target. Colorful yet eye catching.

I kept thinking to myself — how did I get here? How did I end up back in my hometown which I vowed never to move back to again? How did I not see the signs? Why did I stay with this crazy, horrible piece of shit that didn't care about anyone but himself? (That's putting it nicely.) How did I end up in a women's shelter with my 2-year-old son? That wasn't supposed to happen to me!

I remember it was February of 2009. I was 29 and started a new job. I didn't notice "C" at first but after a while he would make an effort to talk to me and flirt. We worked in the same place. I was not in a good place with my self-esteem having just gotten out of my first ever abusive relationship of two years about eight months prior. I started going out with some of my co-workers and a few times C came out too. He started to get flirtier and more friendly. He asked me if he could cook dinner for me at his house some-time. He wanted to cook steaks on the grill. He bought me flowers. He definitely said and did all the right things. He was six years younger than me so there was some hesitation at first because I didn't date guys younger than me.

He went on to surprise me with purple roses (ironically my favorite color since I was a child) in my car after work. Took me out to dinner, and laid on the compliments. After a few months I started to stay at his place a lot. It was great. Then four months after dating, I discovered I was pregnant with my son. It definitely was not planned. We got married on Christmas Eve at the courthouse with close family and friends. It was nowhere near the wedding of my dreams. Looking back on it, I remember he couldn't even look me in the eyes when he said his vows.

Everything was great until I went on maternity leave. This was in March 2010. Money was tight with me not working. I hadn't been at the job long enough to even get a partial disability. He wanted to smoke weed (that was his thing). He didn't have any money because he was paying the bills. He picked a huge fight with me and backhanded me in the nose. He cracked it and it was bleeding.

I never went to the hospital. He didn't even feel bad about it either. I was numb, I was in shock. I had a newborn baby and I didn't know what to do. I had lost my grandfather to a heart attack right before Christmas of 2009. He was my rock. I hadn't fully grieved him. I was dealing with postpartum depression and C would pick fights with me. He would hit me, push me down the steps, put me down, throw me on the ground, kick me while I was on the ground. I guess I thought because I had a child, I was hoping he would change.

> *Looking back on it now, my prior abusive relationship pretty much crushed my self-esteem and I settled for the horrible excuse of a human being in C, my ex-husband.*

I didn't really know what to do or what I was feeling except numb. No one really knew about my home life. I later found out that he made me out to be the crazy one at work to our co-workers. All the while he was the crazy one abusing me. I would go into work quiet and withdrawn and my co-workers couldn't understand the change in me. They could tell I wasn't happy, but all the while I was supposedly the one being argumentative. He didn't keep me from all my friends and family like the ex did in my previous relationship.

Eventually the abuse escalated to the point that he punched me so hard in the jaw that my tooth went through my lip. I landed on the floor in a haze of confusion with blood dripping from my chin area. I was definitely out of it and I wouldn't be surprised if I had a concussion. The minute he realized what he did, he went and got a washcloth while apologizing profusely. The bottom left side of my chin was bruised for weeks. I never got any stitches. I do have a small scar there now but you can't see it unless you're up close to me. His mother asked me what happened and I told her I fell down the steps drunk. She said, "Are you sure it wasn't C? I know he's been known to hit girls."

He was surprisingly good with our son and very loving towards him. He never laid a hand on him. It was weird. His oldest son Daniel (this is not his real name) lived with us and he treated him completely different. He had custody. Daniel's mom was not stable and drug addicted. The sad part is that Daniel had behavioral and emotional problems. It didn't help that C beat him when he was bad. I tried to intervene several times. When I did, I got pushed to the ground, shoved up against a wall, or hit.

Eventually C would wait until I was at work to punish Daniel by beating him. I had to keep Daniel home from school one day because he had bruises. A couple of years after I left my ex-husband, he beat Daniel so badly he ran away to his mom's in the same town one half hour away. Abuse was found by CYS in that county and Daniel was placed with his mother. My ex husband only got a slap on the wrist and didn't do any jail time which is absolutely ridiculous.

C is a very violent person. Especially if he doesn't get his own way. He's like an emotionally stunted child in a grown man's body. He unfortunately comes from a dysfunctional family from both of his parents.

**He is a third generation abuser on his paternal side
of the family. His grandfather and great grandfather
were abusive and dysfunctional.**

His mother has battled drug and alcohol addiction for years. She was beaten by his stepfather and so was he. You would think some-one would want to break that cycle, but he is so selfish, greedy, entitled, and without a conscience. He is the poster child for the narcissistic abuser. Nothing was ever his fault either.

We moved to the southwest Reading, Pennsylvania area in 2011 when my son was just over a year old to make a new start. I really thought things would change, but they never did. I left him once in the summer of 2011. I moved to my mom's house with my son for three months. The one day he called me and while I was on the phone he kicked in my son's wooden crib. He did this because I told him I wasn't coming back. I could hear the wood splitting and breaking. He then sent me a picture of it to my email. I was beside myself. He also threatened to kill himself if I didn't come back. I eventually went back to try to make things work. We didn't even live there a full year and I decided it was time to make my escape.

As I was sitting in the counselor's office, I started to have flashbacks of all the times he hit me and threw me around the room like a rag doll when I tried to fight back. How he would throw me on the floor, kick me like a stuffed animal as I would try to get up. How he would push me so hard from behind as I tried to walk away from him so my chin and face would smack off the floor. How he would spit into my face like a snake spitting venom.

How he would call me names, put me down and degrade me until I didn't feel like a human being anymore.

To the point I didn't think I had any dignity left. "You're a horrible mother." "You're lazy." "You'll never go back to school." "Look at you with your makeup on. You look like a clown." "If you won't sleep with me, someone else will." "You can't even keep it together." "You're not stable." "You're crazy." "You're bipolar." The list goes on and on. Imagine a drill sergeant in your face yelling and screaming these things. That's what some days felt like.

Then I had the nerve to do what I only thought about for the past year and one half. I remember it vividly like it all happened yesterday. I came home from the bank. I was supposed to wire money from my bank account to his so he could pay a bill that was directly coming out of his checking account. We had separate accounts because he was financially abusive and I did not trust him with money. He was always making excuses as to why he couldn't pay the bills or spend his money so that I would have to pay the bills. I was not about to let the bills fall behind and get the utilities shut off with kids.

I was laying on the couch and watching a Disney movie with my

2-year-old son Dominic. Suddenly my husband came darting down the stairs like the house was on fire. He then threw his cell phone at my stomach so hard I thought my rib cracked. He started insanely yelling profanities at me. He claimed I didn't wire enough money into his account and continued on and on. I sat up as I was still feeling sore from the phone hitting my ribs and he proceeded to ask me if I was retarded. He told me the amount he needed and that's what I wired. He was the one that told me the wrong amount, but of course it was all my fault, as always.

I don't really know what came over me except that I intuitively hit my breaking point and saw a way out — finally.

I got up, left my son to play in the living room and went upstairs. I grabbed two small duffle bags, packed diapers, wipes, clothes for Dominic and my work clothes. I ran down the steps. I grabbed a couple toys and then put shoes and a coat on Dominic. Everything was a blur and the walls in the wooden panel living room seemed to be closing in on me. My husband was two rooms away in the kitchen. He was still yelling about how I screwed up wiring the money. I was standing in our small living room where the front door was located. I told him I was leaving and my friend from work was coming to get us.

He told me not to think about taking either of the two vehicles we owned. On that note I looked up and saw the keys to the maroon Eddie Bauer Expedition and quietly grabbed them on top of the tv stand. I grabbed my confused son with two bags on my shoulder, walked out of the front door and crossed the narrow street lined with parked cars over to the overly-sized beast of an SUV. My hands were full with a toddler and bags, but I grabbed for the keys in my pocket and hit the unlock button.

I looked up and the sun was shining as brightly as the white snow on the ground. I put my son down in front of the back car door behind the driver's seat so I could get everything opened. Then I hurled the two bags onto the backseat floor, picked up my son and as fast as I could put him in his green and brown car seat decorated with elephants. I buckled his top buckle leaving the bottom unhooked. Next I shut the door, got in the passenger's side, and took off as fast as I could. I never felt so sick to my stomach with panic, anxiety, and fear. It felt like it was all rolled up into one ball in the pit of my stomach.

I sped through the next few blocks through the maze of streets. As soon as I felt far enough away, I pulled over and put the car in park. I looked back at Dominic in his car seat and he had a look of confusion on his face as if he could tell something was wrong. Then it hit me like waves crashing onto rocks and I proceeded to cry hysterically. I called the local police station for the number to the nearest women's shelter. I then called the women's shelter and I was hysterical. The kind, patient woman gave me the address and I plugged it into the navigator app on my phone.

I took one deep breath, wiped away the wave of water on my face, and proceeded to drive off to what I hoped would finally be safety.

After almost a month at Safe Berks Women's Shelter in Reading, Pennsylvania, my family helped my son and I move back to my hometown two hours away. C moved back to his hometown which was one half hour from mine. He then moved to my town eight months later and filed for 50/50 custody. My family helped me get a lawyer and we were able to start out with supervised visits at the suggestion of my lawyer. Unfortunately, biological parents have rights whether we like it or not. He antagonized me at every hearing in front of the judge over his supervised visits. Eventually, he showed up at my job with my son during one of his visitations and my son saw me and ran to me. Keep in mind he was 2 ½ years old.

I immediately called the state police (which weren't much help). A magistrate who is a friend of the family told my relative to take me to the local sheriff's office the next day. They picked him up on his sixth violation of Protection From Abuse (PFA). (He had four in Berks County and this was his second in my hometown). He ended up doing three months in jail and after that he was not in a stable place to live so he dropped the custody. Then a few months later out of nowhere he moved to Florida with another woman and that's where he has been. I have not heard from him, thank God! Of course he has had at least two other victims and with one he had a kid. She eventually left him too and that was the last I heard. That all happened in 2013.

At that time I noticed there were not a lot of pages on Facebook that addressed domestic violence or healing. I found a few pages that helped me with the healing process, but then decided to start my own called **Damsels~N~Distress**. My goal was to provide information for victims/survivors of domestic violence and sexual assault. I didn't really understand what was happening to me when it was happening so I wanted to provide more information for others to understand what abusers do and how. I then expanded to provide information on resources, healing, self-esteem, hope, narcissistic abusive behavior and articles relating to these topics. I'm now at more than 13,000 followers.

I have also built an advocacy platform on LinkedIn and have had not only women, but businessmen reach out too. You see abuse doesn't just happen to women and children. It happens to men too. I also found that the men weren't just abused by other women, but also by co-workers. Yes! You read that right. It happens in the workplace too. I have been able to provide both men and women with resources. I hope to grow my advocacy work to continue to help those in need.

Fast forward to eight years later —
my son and I are doing great!

I have my own place, he's in fifth grade at a local elementary school, and I decided to go back to school myself, majoring in Criminal Justice at the local university.

Prior to going back to school, I had the privilege of working at the local women's center that helped me at one time. Two years after being a client I went through the interview process and became the Prevention Educator (with no teaching degree). I loved my job and I spent a lot of time doing programs and collaborating with a few professors from the local university I now attend. I consider my time at the women's center a stepping stone to where I am now and where I will be headed with my advocacy work. My hopes are to become a victim-witness advocate because I know what it's like to have to face your abuser in court. It feels like you are being traumatized all over again. I'm also thinking about applying to graduate school to become a licensed clinical counselor. I graduated with my bachelor's in Criminal Justice in the summer of 2021.

I'm not telling you that it will be easy to leave and that times won't be tough, but what I hope you get from my story is that you can leave and you can get your freedom back. It may not happen overnight, but it will happen. You can go on to live a positive, abuse-free life. You can accomplish your dreams!

Don't ever let them make you think that you can't or that you are not worth it because you are! You are capable of doing anything you set your mind to. Healing takes time and it will vary for anyone who leaves and starts over. It will be painful, it will hurt, it will be hard. But over time you find yourself again and begin to grow into the person you were meant to be all along.

You may shoot me with your words,
you may cut me with your eyes,
you may kill me with your hatefulness.
But still, like air, I rise.

~ Maya Angelou

Rodelyn Daguplo from Melbourne Australia
Photographed by Angelito Valdez Jr.

Who Would Have Thought?

I have always been a high achiever and well-educated woman. I graduated as valedictorian of my high school. I was on the Dean's List in college in 2004 from Western Mindanao State University, Philippines. I was a teacher. I received the Service Award, Leadership Award and Demonstrator of Teaching Award. In addition, I earned a diploma from TMG College in Australia and am currently working as a disability support practitioner.

I was working full time as a teacher when I met my ex-husband. My mum just died and I missed her terribly. I felt sad and miserable. I was the breadwinner for my four siblings. I was vulnerable. We met when my friend signed me up on an online dating site. I was unsure at first, as I heard some men aren't nice online. But I gave it a go anyway. A few men contacted me but he caught my attention. He seemed genuine and was very handsome.

We chatted for a few months before he came to visit me in person in the Philippines. He was recently divorced and I thought he was the man of my dreams. He was very tall and had a great physique. He seemed nice and so did his parents when I chatted with them online. I fell in love with him. I thought we would grow old together.

After our first couple years of marriage, his true colors began to show. One time during an argument, he got so angry he threw a landline phone at me and the wire hit my face, almost getting my eye. I was upset and I cried for a while but eventually got over it because I thought it was my fault for making him upset. I did not know about domestic violence. I was a naive and innocent young lady from the Philippines and had freshly arrived in Australia. We also were living with my ex-husband's parents in Melbourne.

When we met, he wasn't working, didn't receive much from his divorce settlement and didn't have a house or savings. I was working two jobs after four months of being in Australia. I worked in the nursing home on weekends as an assistant nurse and during the weekdays as a kinder teacher and qualified staff in the before-and-after school care program. I have no memory of him cooking a meal for me after working long days. I barely had a day off as I was saving for the deposit on our first house. We paid his parents rent and some of the bills. I didn't mind helping. He was living on a Newstart allowance from the government while studying to get his white card as a certified welder, and building a welding business.

Between my two jobs I managed to save a deposit for our first house in Melbourne. It was his dream to live closer to the beach. He applied for a credit card in his name for the remaining amount of the deposit. Then I discovered later, that after we had the house, he borrowed money from that mortgage to pay off his credit card.

We also borrowed money from the new mortgage
to pay for his balance on a car loan
which he still owed from his second divorce.
I didn't realize I was being financially abused.

After we moved into our new house everything was smooth for a while. However, sometimes we would get into an argument because he would refuse to pick me up or drop me off to work. I had to walk at least 45 minutes to get to work. I had to wake up extra early to get to work on time and sometimes walked in the freezing cold weather. I was too shy to ask for a lift from my co-workers and there wasn't a taxi service available. When I finished working my second job in the evenings at a restaurant, I also walked home late at night.

On one occasion I purchased an iPhone using my own money and I didn't tell him. He picked up my brand new phone and threw it on the floor destroying it. My heart ached that he didn't acknowledge the time and effort I put in for our family. Instead he ruined what I had purchased to reward myself. Every time I went somewhere he asked me,"What are you buying now?" "Are you spending money on bags and shoes again?" "You just love wasting more money!"

At times when we argued in the car he would call me a "bitch," "cunt," "stupid," any name he could think of and drive the car so fast either losing control or almost hitting another car just to scare me.

I felt intimidated and depressed from his behaviors and wondered if it was a normal part of his culture.

After our oldest son was born he hardly helped me look after him unless I begged him. I did everything in the house and with the kids. Plus I worked a night shift. He stayed in the garage and did whatever he wanted to do. He came inside to eat dinner and get ready for bed. Sometimes I hardly had any sleep after taking care of the kids during the day and then working a night shift up until my second child was born. I worked up until 32 weeks of pregnancy with both kids so I could pay our bills. Both children were born at 34 weeks through an emergency Cesarean and planned Cesarean due to gestational diabetes. Luckily, they both are healthy.

The worst abuse happened on the day of my daughter's first birthday and Christening celebration on January 15, 2017. My ex-husband almost killed me. I informed him that I planned to spend the same amount of money I spent on our son's party. I saved all of it and he did not contribute anything. He was so grumpy knowing I spent that much money on something important to me.

He was late for the Christening ceremony and birthday and was very rude to our guests. I asked him to move my car since I parked in a 15-minute parking zone at the venue to hurry in with my two kids. Instead, he hid my car in a corner where it was hard to find without telling me where it was parked. On top of that, he left early, leaving me with the two kids looking for the car for ages. I called him many times but no answer. I was so tired already, I was up the night before preparing plus taking care of the two children by myself without any help from him. I was lucky my daughter's Godfather helped me pack up the venue after the party and dropped off the party supplies at my place. He also helped me look for my car with two tired kids who were crying by then.

I was exhausted and got home about 10 p.m. I was very upset at his immaturity and rudeness. I was breastfeeding our daughter on the couch while watching TV to relax before putting the kids to bed. Our son was sitting on the couch next to me watching TV before going to bed. He started yelling at me calling me names, saying I was stupid for spending too much money and lying to him about how much I spent. He was pointing his finger at me and yelling. I told him to "back up" and he had no right to control how much I spent on our daughter's party since I saved my own money for that party.

And he did not share any expense for the party nor did he put any effort in to help me prepare. In fact, he ruined it. I told him I had enough with his attitude and I was leaving him. He got so mad and came toward me after I asked him to back up. I kicked him and he grabbed my feet and dragged me on the carpet toward the kitchen, lifted me up by my feet and dropped me to the floor on my head.

Everything went dark for a few minutes. I was shaking and scared, in a panic. I got up and ran towards the phone. I managed to get the phone but he tackled me and grabbed the phone so I couldn't dial 000 to reach the police. I ran for the car keys and toward the main door. He tackled me again and pushed the keys so hard into my hand I began bleeding.

My kids saw everything happening and were on the couch crying, so I went to pick them up.

Luckily, I put down our daughter on the couch before he could get to me, ran for the spare room, pushed the bed against the door and called 000. The police arrived and investigated. My son told the police, "My poor mummy. Daddy was very angry. Daddy lifted her feet up high and dropped her. Then mum cried."

My heart broke into pieces after hearing my son talking to the police. My innocent young son, 2 ½ years old, was so brave to speak up and tell the truth. My ex-husband twisted the story so he would look good. He said that he got angry at me for financial issues. He said that I was hiding money behind his back while he was working full time and I was only working casually on a night shift. He said

I was kicking him and he was just defending himself. He is such a liar. I was working two jobs and used a babysitter sometimes because he didn't help me and stayed in the garage doing whatever he was doing.

The ambulance arrived on the scene and the paramedics checked my injuries. I was given an Endone for the pain in my back and they suggested I go to the hospital. But I refused because no one would look after my kids and I was scared of what could happen during the night. I took the pain medications and endured the rest, telling them I would see my doctor in the morning. When I went he confirmed that I suffered a soft tissue injury to my spine. I took anti-inflammation medication and improved. I also received help from Safe Step. The case manager visited me and ensured I had the list for emergency evacuation just in case my ex attacked me again. I ended up relying on Safe Step, a family violence response center, to guide me through until I decided to leave.

The police officer asked me that night if
I wanted to press charges. I looked at my kids,
felt sorry for them and I told the police officer
that I didn't want to charge him.

I would be ok. I was thinking of my kids and how they would handle it if their father went to jail. They loved him. He was taken by the police and an Intervention Order (IVO) was issued for him that night. He breached it a few times until I applied for an indefinite IVO and a judge approved it for a lifetime until January 2060, because of the extent he went through to defy the original one.

The abuse continued despite an IVO in place. We lived together but in separate bedrooms for the sake of the kids. I remembered he grabbed my very expensive Louis Vuitton bag valued at $2,700 and put it in the mud. He ruined it and laughed at me saying, "Look at your expensive bag. It's swimming in the mud." I was so upset. I worked so hard to pay for that bag as a reward for myself and he ruined it. Sometimes before I went to work, he would grab my keys and hide them so I would be late, not able to work or get in trouble. I used to get so upset at all his immaturity and abuse. He tried to control me as much as he could. When I decided I had enough with him and ended the relationship, he said to me, "No one will ever love you. You are very bad in bed, you have saggy boobs, a fat tummy and are a psycho. No man will ever love you."

That stuck in my brain and I lost confidence in myself. When I had enough and said we couldn't fix our marriage, he decided to find someone online to replace me even though I was still living at our home. So I also decided to look at online dating too. I found someone from overseas. One day he asked me to send him a photo of the guy that I was chatting with online because he wanted to know what he looked like. I was innocent and trusted him and sent the picture. I did not know he was planning something bad and would use it against me to ruin my reputation. He sent that man's photo to all my friends and family on Facebook, claiming that I broke up with him because I cheated on him. It was his way of covering up his domestic violence in our marriage.

I felt so ashamed. He ruined my reputation.
Some of my friends and family believed him and
I ended up looking like I cheated on my husband
which I did not.

After our online relationship broke up, that man ended up being a scammer and took $12,000 Australian dollars from me. My husband laughed when he heard I got scammed. But I learned my lesson the hard way after that man kept promising me a fairy tale life and asking me to send him money overseas. I was so weak and vulnerable.

In the meantime, my ex-husband continued to break the IVO order. The last incident was December 2020 when he came to my house, blocked my driveway with his car and a trailer, and threw some keys at me screaming that I was a thief for stealing the key to his safe. He eventually found out that his parents were the ones who took his key and replaced it with their spare key for him. I was so scared and frightened. I ended up calling 000 to report the IVO breach as my kids were in the car when that incident happened.

It took four years for him to give me my share of money for the house and I needed to pay a huge amount for my lawyer's fee. In the end I received less than my share because I was always concerned about how it affected my kids. But he obviously took advantage of my kindness and generosity. If I had my way, I would not wish to see him anymore. Seeing him during the kids' drop offs and pick ups still gives me anxiety and brings back bad memories.

The abuse from my ex-husband really affected my self-esteem. Every time I looked in the mirror the hateful words he used to describe me were stuck in my mind. I had issues sleeping. In my nightmares my ex was chasing me trying to kill me and some times even burying me alive. I was so anxious, restless and scared of the dark. I always locked my doors.

I also was stressed with my divorce, trying to fit my work hours with my kids' pick up and dropoff from school. I also worked week-ends when my children were with their father. He wanted weekend visitation so he didn't have to manage the school schedule and they all could sleep in. As usual, he hardly did anything with the kids and continued to do his own thing in the garage.

One time I was so upset I was planning to end everything and jump off the pier in the middle of the night when no one would know.

When I was walking towards the pier to do it, I felt the cold air blowing on my face. I suddenly remembered my late mum's teaching, "No matter how hard life can be, there is a rainbow at the end of the rain." She also said, "There is light at the end of the tunnel." And I remembered the priest teaching that committing suicide is a big sin and I would go to hell. I turned back, went to my car and cried. I asked for forgiveness from God and strength that I would not try it again. I felt lost and miserable.

Since then I have reached out to God and attended Hill Song Christian Church in Knoxfield with my relative/very close friend and her husband's family. I surrendered my life to God and I was in tears most of that service. Every word the preacher said just made me cry and touched my soul. I wrote my prayer request and the church members prayed for me. I felt like I was home and found hope. Since then I put myself together and continue to fight for my new life.

After 11 years of marriage and two more years of living with a man who physically and psychologically abused me, we finally parted ways. I chose to stay that long because I couldn't find the right help. I was ashamed to tell anyone I was suffering, even after we broke up. I hoped for the sake of our kids, he would change for the better. But he only got worse. There was not a day without fighting in front of the kids. I learned to fight back and called the police more.

Then he said to me, "Well, if you can't forgive me for what I did, I can easily replace you. There are a lot of desperate women in the Philippines that will marry me and they look the same as you." He ended up finding a woman from the same town with the same similarities and figure as me. He would talk to her on speaker in an attempt to make me jealous.

I just kept quiet and inside I felt hurt that he could move on so easily after 11 years. It's like I had an open wound and he poured salt in it.

When my ex-husband decided to meet his new girlfriend in the Philippines it was perfect timing for me to move out. He went on a holiday for two weeks and I managed to find a rental home. I only took the TV which I paid for and the kids' beds. I managed to buy the furniture I needed. My friend and my boss lent me some money for my rent. I paid them back as soon as I could. I wasn't qualified for government support since I was working. I am forever grateful for their financial support during that difficult time in my life. Then Anglicare Victoria took over to help me get through our transition and guided me with the IVO and a financial settlement. Their services for children also helped my son cope with his trauma, setting up therapy sessions. In addition, they arranged art therapy for my daughter along with relaxation massage and yoga sessions for me.

Being a single mum was hard in the beginning and I was worried how I was going to survive. I was in pain and I was lost but I did not give up. I managed to continue to work and I hired a babysitter when I went to work. It was very hard working night shifts and staying awake when I dropped them off to kinder and daycare until both of them went to primary school.

It was difficult to handle the hard times. I knew there was a better way to deal with my problems. I surrendered myself to God and I trusted God to guide me. I continued to work my two jobs at the nursing home and in disability. I learned to take better care of myself. I enrolled in a yoga class and I joined the gym. I am glad we survived the hardest part of my life.

To build my self-confidence, I attended the Charity Beauty Pegeant. I was chosen 2nd Runner-Up in the Philippine Fiesta of Victoria Inc. Queen and Charity pageant in 2018. I was nominated by the Face Australia Pageantry as Mrs. International Asian Mum of the Year Mindanao, Philippines 2019. Meanwhile, I went to Singapore to compete in the International Asian Mum of the Year competition in the Asia Pacific Beauty Fashion and Friendship Festival 2019. I gained my international title as Mrs. Timeless Beauty Ambassador of Earth 2019. I also became the International Asian Mum of the Year 2019 Ambassador.

I currently hold the Mrs. Universe Pacific Islands title. For all of my success, I was featured as the "Cover Queen" in the World Class Beauty Queens Magazine Issue 123, January 2021. I also started my own online businesses, Queen Lyn Travel & Tours, and Health & Beauty by Queenlyn. I am so excited to be part of this book, #SheWins 2 by Alisa Divine. On December 5, 2021, I will compete in Mrs.Universe in Seoul, South Korea.

*During my four years as a single mum,
I've been better off financially
than when I was with my ex-husband.*

I even manage to continue my charity work sharing my blessings with others in the small ways that I can. I donated clothes and money to feed the unfortunate children in the Philippines. I managed to help victims and survivors of domestic violence to buy petrol, groceries and emergency accommodations because I know what it is like to be in their shoes. I have helped a few women by letting them stay in our spare bedroom as an emergency accommodation until the government helped them or they were ready to stand on their own. I also guided them on the next steps and referred them to the right agency for support. I also managed to help international students in Melbourne by giving them cash to buy and deliver groceries to those affected by the COVID 19 Pandemic.

I share because God has blessed me in so many ways.
As my late mum taught me,
"It is better to give than to receive."

I am also the 2020-2021 president of the Women's Association, Inc. It began when some women gathered and we talked about struggles with divorce and domestic violence. We thought we would create a charity group to help women with emergency rent assistance and grocery vouchers. These charity officers and members witnessed all my struggles and how I survived. They were there for me, listened to me, comforted me and inspired me to continue to fight for what I am entitled to and to stand up for my rights as a woman. The association helps women, children, elderly and disabled people with support in any situation. Our intent is to protect, empower, outsource, provide, lead and encourage women.

After I broke away from my ex husband, I refused to date any man that had a similar attitude. As soon as I saw a red flag from a man I dated, I told him right away that he was not the one I was looking for. I set high standards for my next partner after a few failed relationships and I actually had a checklist so I would not fall for a narcissistic man again. I failed a few times after my ex husband but I did not give up.

After some time on my own, I found my current partner. He treats me well and he seems genuine with me. I met his family and his friends and I am really happy when I am with him. He is a very down to earth man, generous, caring, sweet and thoughtful. He is the man of my dreams and my true love. He helped put my broken pieces together. He was there when I was in a mess and never left my side despite how much I pushed him away due to my past. He treats me like a queen and spoils me in so many ways. I feel so lucky having him in my life.

My message to all my fellow survivors is — don't lose hope. I found someone who is deserving of my love. I'm sure someone out there is waiting for you. I want other women to know that there is help and they are not alone. It is hard to leave a toxic relationship and it is hard to recover from trauma and start fresh, but once you get the hang of it you will be fine. Everything will fall in its place. I did it. You can do it too.

Please don't suffer in silence. Find the courage to speak up and ask for help. Be aware of the red flags. Our life is too short to waste it in a toxic relationship. All women deserve to be treated with respect and dignity by our partners. We all deserve to be happy. But it is up to us how we teach our partner to treat us.

Recently I purchased a new home. I turned my pain into power. I look at all the struggles that I have been through with my ex husband and use them as an inspiration to do better in life and to work harder to achieve my dreams. I use my pains to fight and get through my everyday life. They are also a learning tool as I face my future. I always look at the silver lining in bad situations. I also always believe what my mum told me — "There is a rainbow at the end of the rain" and "a light at the end of the tunnel."

I know that time heals all wounds.

My mother would take the Band-Aid off,
clean the wound, and say,
"Things that are covered don't heal well."
Mother was right.
Things that are covered do not heal well.

~ T.D. Jakes

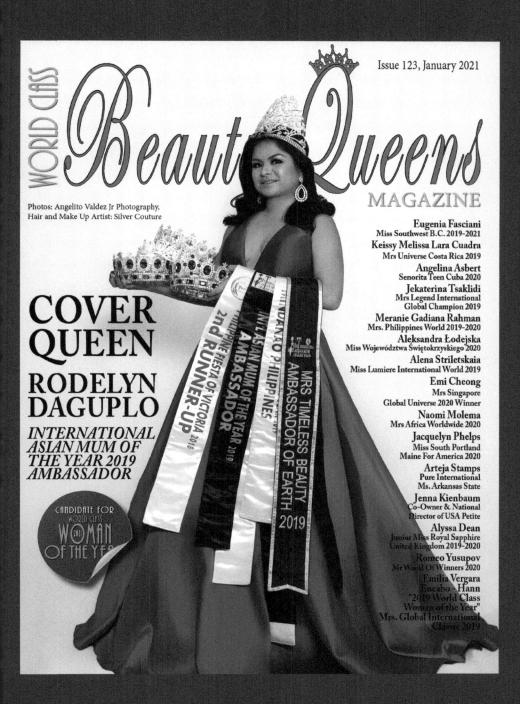

Issue 123, January 2021

WORLD CLASS

Beauty Queens

MAGAZINE

Photos: Angelito Valdez Jr Photography,
Hair and Make Up Artist: Silver Couture

Eugenia Fasciani
Miss Southwest B.C. 2019-2021

Keissy Melissa Lara Cuadra
Mrs Universe Costa Rica 2019

Angelina Asbert
Senorita Teen Cuba 2020

Jekaterina Tsaklidi
Mrs Legend International
Global Champion 2019

Meranie Gadiana Rahman
Mrs. Philippines World 2019-2020

Aleksandra Łodejska
Miss Województwa Świętokrzyskiego 2020

Alena Striletskaia
Miss Lumiere International World 2019

Emi Cheong
Mrs Singapore
Global Universe 2020 Winner

Naomi Molema
Mrs Africa Worldwide 2020

Jacquelyn Phelps
Miss South Portland
Maine For America 2020

Arteja Stamps
Pure International
Ms. Arkansas State

Jenna Kienbaum
Co-Owner & National
Director of USA Petite

Alyssa Dean
Junior Miss Royal Sapphire
United Kingdom 2019-2020

Romeo Yusupov
Mr World Of Winners 2020

**Emilia Vergara
Encabo - Hann**
"2019 World Class
Woman of the Year"
Mrs. Global International
Classic 2019

COVER QUEEN

RODELYN DAGUPLO

INTERNATIONAL ASIAN MUM OF THE YEAR 2019 AMBASSADOR

CANDIDATE FOR
WORLD CLASS
WOMAN
OF THE YEAR

Brandy Reese Sloan from Texas

From Broken Hands To Helping Hands

I suffered in silence. For many years.

Beginning with my first serious relationship in college and in each subsequent relationship I had until I was in my thirties, I minimized and rationalized away the abuse I suffered at the hands of multiple partners. I never thought of myself as a "victim of domestic violence." I didn't know that those words applied to me. I didn't know that what was happening to me was considered abuse. I didn't know that even the occasional hit or slap was still assault. I didn't know I was allowed to say "no" if they wanted to have sex and I didn't.

I usually blamed myself — if I could just "be better," then he wouldn't get so angry. He wouldn't have to slap me or kick me or shove me. I thought if I could just change and be the perfect woman he wanted, then he wouldn't do those things. I thought it was all my fault. These are the lies that domestic violence wants us to believe.

So I went from one abusive situation to the next, carrying this sickness of domestic violence with me as it grew bigger and more toxic — until the final act of violence that nearly ended my life.

On August 22, 2010, the man I was in a relationship with at the time, beat me nearly to death with an aluminum baseball bat and strangled me until he thought I was dead. I remember him coming into the bedroom at 3 a.m. As usual, he was blind drunk and he yanked me up out of bed by my hair. He was yelling, accusing me yet again of cheating on him, even though of course I had never done anything of the sort. I decided I had had enough of him and told him so. I told him I was leaving. And he answered by balling up his fist and punching me in the face, breaking my nose. Then he punched me again, causing a fracture in my jaw.

Then he picked up the bat. I had kept an aluminum baseball bat in the closet for years — ironically, it was supposed to be for protection from intruders. He picked up that bat and hit me in the head as hard as he could, and I saw stars. He hit me again and again. I couldn't count how many times. He brought that bat down over and over while I tried to curl into as small a ball as I could to protect my head. I didn't know it at the time, but my skull was fractured and there was a subdural hematoma on my brain.

I remember being dizzy. I was trying to balance on a floor that was moving and tilting like a ship deck in a storm.

My ears were ringing and I couldn't seem to think straight. All I felt was fear. All I knew was terror. I couldn't even really feel the pain. He threw down the bat, which was bent in the middle from hitting me so hard and then, unbelievably, things got even worse. He got on top of me, wrapped both hands around my neck and squeezed. I struggled for air, my blood running in rivers down my face, stinging my eyes. I kept clawing at his hands, realizing in confusion that my hands wouldn't work. That's when I noticed my fingers were mangled and my arms were bent at odd angles. He had broken both of my arms and crushed my hands. All but three of my fingers were broken. Still, I couldn't feel the pain.

He kept choking me, over and over — he would squeeze until I felt like my head and chest were going to explode, then he'd let up for a fraction of a second. Then, before I had a chance to draw a breath, he'd squeeze again, harder. He looked me right in the face while he did this. I looked into his eyes and they were completely black, as if he had no soul. He knew he was killing me and still, he kept on strangling me.

I think I lost consciousness because the next thing I remember I was laying on the floor and he was crouching like a child in the corner, crying, and mumbling incoherently in his native language. I think he must have thought I was dead because at some point he just got up and left the room, leaving me in a large, sticky pool of my own blood.

At that moment, I looked over and saw my cell phone on the floor.

I managed to crawl to it and somehow, with my destroyed hands, dialed 911. Unable to hold the phone, I laid it next to my head and begged the dispatcher to send someone to help me.

I remember begging her, her, "Please don't hang up" and she promised she'd stay on the phone with me until help arrived. He came back into the room then and was standing over me while I begged the dispatcher, "Please send someone fast." It seemed like just moments later when the police arrived, took one look at him covered in my blood and immediately placed him under arrest. The paramedics arrived soon after.

I still get chills when I think of how close I came to death.

It is quite telling that he used the bat to break my hands. I'm a musician. I've played piano and taught lessons nearly all my life. Injuring my hands was the worst way possible to hurt me — and he knew that. Also, I was in the early stages of pregnancy and unfortunately my unborn child did not survive. Not a day goes by that I don't think of that lost baby.

That final incident of violence was by far the worst I had ever experienced. The relationship wasn't always like that — in the beginning he was so sweet and charming, until he wasn't. Gradually, and insidiously, the abuse started, then escalated, before I even knew what was happening to me. It started with comments about my outfit, my makeup — "why did I need to wear that, who was I trying to impress? I must have someone on the side…" He was always accusing me of cheating, or flirting with someone — but I never did anything to even suggest I would do that, I wouldn't.

And how could I anyway? He never let me out of his sight. The jealousy, the accusations eventually graduated to restraining me and holding me in rooms, not letting me out, every day accusing me of sleeping with someone behind his back or some other sin I hadn't committed. He hadn't hit me yet — but the emotional and verbal abuse was almost constant. And the drinking. Always drinking. He could drink entire cases of beer by himself. He drank to the point of passing out and wetting the bed most nights. Then he would wake up in a wet dirty bed and yell at me to clean it up.

Finally, one day in August, I had enough. I told him I was leaving. He stood behind my car, trying to keep me from pulling away. I had to maneuver the car and jump a curb just to get away. I went and stayed at a friend's house while I tried to figure out what I was going to do. I had no money, no job, and no place to live. He had made me totally dependent on him. After calling and texting me constantly for days, he finally talked me into coming over to discuss things.

He promised things would be better, that he would change, he was so sorry, he loved me so much. I fell for it.

I didn't feel like I had a choice — I had no resources, where was I going to go? And I loved him, I did. I wanted my relationship to work. I wanted so badly to believe him when he said things would be better. And for exactly one week — they were better. On August 22, everything changed. On August 22, he tried to murder me when I told him I was leaving for good.

That terrifying night on August 22, 2010 was ironically how I finally broke free from domestic violence. It finally broke the cycle I'd been living in for so many years. While recovering in the hospital, I got the number of Family Violence Prevention Services, the local domestic violence organization in San Antonio where I live. I found an amazing support group. It was there that I was first educated about domestic violence and where I learned to accept that I was in fact, a victim of abuse. I learned that it was not okay, that I didn't deserve it, and that I didn't have to live that way. I learned valuable lessons and coping skills and how to spot red flags in subsequent relationships.

I began to heal. The ladies I met in my support group are some of the strongest, most courageous women I've ever known. We cried together, we held each other, we built each other up and celebrated our accomplishments. We leaned on each other in ways that nobody who hasn't lived through what we've lived could understand. Many of us are still friends and we still check in on each other, making sure we're all still okay. I had surgery and physical therapy to get my hands back. I began playing music again.

Then I began to rebuild my life. I became a victim's advocate, working with various domestic violence organizations. I started telling my story, speaking my truth in the hopes that I could help others find their way out of their own dark places. I found my voice and then with my fellow survivor sisters, I lent my voice to others who couldn't speak for themselves. I used it to educate and raise awareness about domestic violence and how people can help. I marched in rallies, I spoke on panels to members of law enforcement and officers of the court. I helped educate aspiring medical professionals in medical school on how to spot signs of abuse and get the victim proper help. I implored members of government to change policy to hold perpetrators of domestic violence accountable for their crimes.

I also spoke in high schools to educate young people who are just beginning their own dating journey.

I told them about what healthy and unhealthy relationships look like, what to do if they are unsafe in their relationship, or at home, and where to find the proper help. I helped raise money for shelters and transitional housing, took up collections of clothing and supplies and I helped spearhead and implement a music program for the children in the local Battered Women's and Children's Shelter. A few times, I even physically helped extract victims from unsafe situations. Giving back and helping others helped me find my strength and gave me a newfound purpose in life. I became ME again.

I even found love again — I am now married to an amazing man who would never dream of hurting me. We have a beautiful life and we own a small music school together where I'm able to teach and play music every day. I have lived my best life in spite of domestic violence. I feel like I was given a second chance at life and I am careful not to waste that gift. I can say with absolute certainty that I won't ever allow myself to be abused again. I am a survivor of domestic violence. I will never again be anyone's victim.

One of the most important parts of my journey toward healing was facing my abuser in court. It took two years, but I was able to see him brought to justice — something not every victim is able to do. The legal process involving domestic violence can be frustrating and complicated. The abuser is often given chance after chance to abuse the victim again, because they aren't properly held accountable for their crimes. Law enforcement doesn't always come in time, they don't always arrest the abuser and way too often the victim is the one who gets blamed. If the abuser does get arrested, they spend so little time in jail, the victim sometimes doesn't have time to get safely away, if they even have somewhere to go. Orders of protection are just pieces of paper. The abuser does not care and will walk right past them to get to the victim.

So many of our sisters who were killed by their abusers had orders of protection on file.

He bonded out of jail within 48 hours, before I even got out of ICU at the hospital. Then he was free on the street for two years until he reached a plea agreement with the court and was finally sentenced. He received a 15-year sentence for his guilty plea. It didn't feel like nearly enough time for killing my unborn child and almost killing me — but I was just so relieved he was finally going to prison that I took it as a win. He was going to be behind bars and at least for the next 15 years I didn't have to worry about him. He became eligible for parole a couple years ago, and every year so far he's been denied. Every year when the time comes around I hold my breath, waiting to hear if they're letting him out. When I find out he's been denied again, citing the violent nature of his crimes, I feel like I did the day of sentencing — like I can breathe a bit easier. I know the day will come when he finishes his sentence and comes out of prison. I am already preparing myself for that day.

Many people have asked me how I could go from one abusive relationship to the next. Why didn't I see it, why didn't I stop it? This is actually very common — it's called revictimization. Predators are good at spotting prey. It's the same with abusers. They find us, over and over again, until we get the proper help and are able to break the cycle.

I've also often heard the question, "why didn't I just leave, or why did I stay?" This seems to be the number one question for every

107

survivor of domestic violence. "Why didn't I just leave?" There are countless answers to this question. The abusive partner often makes it impossible for the victim to leave — either by making them financially dependent upon them or isolating them from family and friends. They do not allow them to form other social relationships, so the victim has nobody to turn to. Financial abuse occurs in 98 percent of abusive relationships and domestic violence is the third leading cause of homelessness among families. The abuser often "gaslights" the victim, making them feel like they're "going crazy," and breaks their self-esteem down so much, they feel they truly have no one, deserve nothing, and nobody would believe them anyway.

He made me financially dependent and cut me off from all the money, so even if I left, I had nothing, and nowhere to go. The only way I finally escaped was in the back of an ambulance and I literally had nothing. I started my life over with only the ripped underwear I was wearing when they brought me to the ER that night — that was all I had to my name. He had isolated me from everyone except him and his family. I wasn't allowed friends and he'd made me alienate myself from my own family. I felt alone. I learned that behavior was typical of an abusive partner.

The abuser often threatens the victim if they "try to leave." And many make good on their threats.

When I finally got up the courage to tell my abuser I was leaving, he responded by trying to murder me. I would later learn that the most dangerous time for a victim of domestic violence is at the end of the relationship. The degree of lethality for the victim goes up exponentially, as much as 70 times, in the days and weeks immediately after leaving the abusive relationship. I stayed because I was stuck.

I didn't know what I would do or where I would go if I left. I wanted so desperately to believe that things could be different. I stayed way longer than I should have, because I didn't know I deserved any better and because "it wasn't so bad" — meaning I'd never had to go to the emergency room before. I didn't think I was "really" being abused. I didn't have a name for what happened but knew it

108

felt awful and I wanted it to stop. It wasn't until I was very nearly murdered that I thought my situation was "bad enough" to reach out for help. This is why I am so passionate now about raising awareness, about helping other women find their way to help before it's too late — because it was almost too late for me.

My story is just one of tens of thousands. Domestic violence is the second leading cause of death for women, preceded only by auto accidents. We actually have a better chance of surviving cancer than we do at surviving an abusive relationship. Bexar County, where I live, was recently named the fourth deadliest county in the state of Texas when it comes to domestic violence. One out of every three women will become a victim of an abusive relationship. In the US, a woman is assaulted or beaten by their intimate partner every nine seconds. More than 3 million children witness domestic violence in their homes every year. Domestic violence has become an epidemic.

The only way to stop the death, to stop the violence, and save lives is with more awareness, with education, with counseling, and with resources for victims to safely leave their abusive situations and start to rebuild their lives. Everyone has the right to live with dignity, free from fear, free from violence, and free from harm. If we all stand together, we can make sure that victims live to be survivors, who not only survive, but thrive.

You may have to fight a battle more than once to win it.

~ Margaret Thatcher

HelenMarie McCracken from Arizona

photographed by Jessica Korff

Trust Your Gut

On my wedding day, May 2001, my daddy told me, "if this doesn't feel right, it's ok not to get married today." I always envisioned sharing my life with the perfect partner, having a big beautiful wedding, creating a happy healthy family, and enjoying everlasting love — love that resembled what my parents exuded. On that day, every ounce of my being was telling me he was the wrong partner for me, yet I went through with it anyway. Ultimately, this was the beginning of my evolution.

From the outside looking in, we appeared to be the perfect All-American family. Yet, on the inside, the reality was much different. Our marriage was full of lies and catastrophes. As his wife, I was doing my due diligence to help and support him with his problems while I suppressed my own. My ex was the catalyst for me to heal nearly 40 years of abuse. Through my healing, I learned the abuse went as far back as when I was in my mother's womb and continued at age 5, when I was sexually abused by my brother, and ended with a violent marriage. For my entire life, I was living in a fight, flight, or freeze mode — unconsciously, making my true self feel alone and isolated as if time stood still.

In 2012, my entire life came to a halt. He moved out of the marital home in April due to his uncontrollable anger and actions. At that time he promised to seek help and do what it would take to be a better husband. He was raised in an unhealthy household and promised he would do better for our family. That was a lie because it sure was not our reality.

In August, at the mere mention of divorce, he became enraged and broke my eye socket. One day following dinner and drinks with a friend, he stopped by the marital home. I told him his actions continued to prove his behavior was not changing and that I wanted a divorce. He angrily stated, "absolutely not! If I can't have you, no one can." He proceeded to walk away. Then he turned back towards me, eyes filled with pure evil.

He lunged at me and punched me in the right eye. His punch was so impactful, I flew back and fell onto the ground, unconscious. When I regained consciousness, I was disorientated and in immense pain. My level of terror had intensified more than ever before. I ran to my children to make sure they were safe.

The next morning, my good friend stopped over, took one look at me, and knew my ex had been there. I pleaded with her to cover for me until I was able to establish a safety plan. She was aware of the severity of this situation because she had witnessed the abuse inflicted by him on numerous occasions. His behavior became increasingly unpredictable and more volatile over the next six months.

In October, after a visit with their father, my children confided to me they were being physically and verbally abused. This piece of news mortified me. I became weary, numb, tired, depleted, and lost. I felt I lived in an empty shell of who I was. Keep in mind during this time, he was taking prescription medication and participating in talk therapy, while attending anger management classes.

When I told my ex I was filing for divorce, he exploded. He was enraged with the mindset of going to war. He came after me with a baseball bat, threatening to kill me in front of the children! I knew then, without a shadow of a doubt, we were no longer safe. This incident gave me the courage to file for divorce (Feb 2013) and apply for an Order of Protection, which was of grave importance to all of us. Through all of this, it was crucial to make sure my children would never be victims of his abuse ever again.

Then began a nearly three-year tortuous battle with the court system that ended unjustly.

Despite the evidence of abuse provided through witnesses, photos, emails, and text messages, the judicial system favored my ex. I was blown away at the outcome. I was haunted by fear and knew it was imperative for us to feel safe and secure once and for all.

Throughout the divorce, I began researching — to better educate myself and I discovered he is a narcissist. Traits of a narcissist are someone who has little or no empathy, manipulates others, gaslights (makes others doubt their reality), lies incessantly, and believes their own lies. They create doubt in your feelings and emotions, then call you crazy. They rage for absolutely no reason until you end up apologizing. I now had answers and no longer felt alone.

At that time I also began seeking out support groups,
both in local areas and through social media.

I learned more about narcissists, domestic violence (physical, emotional, sexual, financial, psychological, technological, and spiritual abuse). I learned that I am an empath, which was a double-edged sword. I was so grateful to learn about Narcissistic Personality Disorder characteristics and empaths as well as domestic violence, child abuse, and generational patterns and behaviors. This gave me a better understanding of what I had been enduring for so many years, why I allowed it to transpire as long as I did, and that domestic violence was more prevalent in every zip code.

My next discovery, was 'The Law of Attraction" from the book *The Secret* by Rhonda Byrne, which offered me a glimmer of hope and a path to follow as the divorce proceedings began. I was afraid for my life because of the previous antics, threats and actions of my ex-husband. In my opinion, the Judicial System created more fear and feelings of worthlessness throughout this process which made me so furious. I was ready to expose the underhanded money games and collusion taking place right before my eyes.

The GAL (Guardian Ad Litem) threatened to take my children away if I were to go public or report anything negative about their system. I approached every legal resource available to me, including writing to the President of The United States of America — with no success. Through my fear, I found, the only option was to use my voice, to speak up to protect my children and myself. Grace was on my side because I retained full custody of my children with the provision of never having contact with their abusive biological father again.

Little did I know, the worst was yet to come. In 2016, seven months after the divorce was final, I found out my son was sexually abused by his biological father. My brave son felt safe enough to disclose this awful fact to his school counselor. The principal and counselor both shared what my son told them. I sat there, speechless and in shock from what I was hearing. I felt as if I was suffocating, and my heart could stop beating at any moment. I trembled, cried uncontrollably, clinched my dislocated jaw while feeling an overwhelming sense of emotions.

When this truth was exposed it created a downward spiral for me and my children.

The school reported this incident to DCFS (Illinois Department of Children & Family Services) and scheduled a visit the same day because they thought my ex-husband was still living with us. Once they found out we were already divorced, they referred us to the Elk Grove Village Police Department Investigators and The Children's Advocacy Center of North & Northwest Cook County for forensic interviews and trauma therapy. In 2016 and 2017, twice, my son endured forensic interviews. To help him feel more comfortable in sharing the details, a trauma therapist as well as various other personnel were provided to him. He disclosed every detail of the abuse; from playing around to inappropriate touching to the full disclosure of physical and sexual abuse forced upon him. In retrospect, I felt mortified for my son. Not only was he subjected to this sexual abuse, but he was also revictimized when he had to relive these traumatic experiences.

Of course, my ex-husband went to the police station with his attorney, denied all allegations, and insisted he was not guilty on all charges of child sexual abuse. I felt depressed and unable to think clearly. Everything that transpired to that point had caused a downward spiral for my entire family. The Elk Grove Police Department referred me to a holistic counselor to help me process and cope with my son's sexual abuse.

After experiencing trials and tribulations with other counselors, this counselor taught me energy healing, mantras, and meditation. We aligned immediately. The courts and more police visits provoked a wave of inner anger and fear that I found hard to control.

I almost lost hope and gave up. But I had to fight for my children! I became my own hero! I started to read self-help books about spiritual and holistic methods of healing. I learned EFT (emotional freedom techniques), how to shift my mindset and shatter my limiting beliefs, and I practiced meditation and yoga.

This journey led me to read the Bible. It guided me closer to God, which was instrumental to my awakening and a better relationship with God. I quickly realized there would be no justice for my son, again. The investigators strongly recommended we move away from Illinois as soon as possible. It was dangerous for us to remain in Illinois because we would never feel safe.

On top of all of the sadness and turmoil, my Mom, who was my best friend and rock, suddenly passed away in September 2016, two days after her 67th birthday. My Mom was by my side through all the trials and tribulations, including the court proceedings. She often told me to move out of the state because my ex-husband violated the Order of Protection and she was afraid for our safety. Her passing ignited a force within me to make a drastic decision for my family. In August 2017, I manifested selling our house, donating unnecessary belongings, and a move to Arizona.

This decision to move cross country took a great deal
of courage and faith for all of us.
It changed the trajectory of our lives.

In January 2018 as my family and I continued to settle into our new life out of nowhere, my life flashed before me when God brought me to my knees with a burst of tears. I was overwhelmed and questioned everything. At that time, I had an epiphany and realized how much my emotions had a rippling effect on my family. Out of that awakening, I felt as if I had been reborn. I thought after finally breaking the generational cycle and escaping that the worst was over. The danger and fear were gone, yet my inner healing journey was far from over. Leaving an abusive relationship does not end when you leave. This is actually the true beginning of your healing journey!

I defined this as my "midlife crisis" and chose to pivot in a new direction. The knowledge, skills and holistic tools I gained over the past decade really helped me heal. That alone wasn't enough to heal all of my complex trauma. At the time, I didn't have the proper tools needed to process and heal the root causes of my wounds. This time I had the tools I needed and completed the "full circle" of healing.

As we go through life, we experience a range of different emotions. Some emotions are dealt with while others we tend to sweep under a rug. We are brought up with the beliefs that we need to "fit in" with society when in reality we are born to stand out. I found facing my inner emotional, spiritual, and psychological wounds was a laborious painful process. I had to completely redefine my self-worth and rewire my brain by evaluating the four decades of abuse and complex trauma I absorbed and suppressed.

Some of the holistic tools I utilized to advance my healing and release the past are listed below:

- I STOPPED – living in denial. I recognized the abuse and understood it was not my fault. Abuse is NEVER the victim's fault, it's ALWAYS the perpetrator's fault. As a victim, it truly hurts to realize and accept others have hurt or betrayed you.

- FORGIVENESS – I learned to forgive and let go of everything and everyone that did not or no longer served my life positively or added sustenance. In a notebook, I journaled my pain,
- accepting my responsibility to every human and situation that had ever wounded me. I forgave them, myself and released it from my mind, body, and soul. Then I burned the papers.

- I FORGAVE MYSELF — for not knowing better at the time. I forgave myself for the survival patterns I implemented while enduring trauma. I forgave myself for not being who I needed to be. I forgave myself for not knowing then what I know now. My greatest lesson is accepting that I cannot change the past, only forgive and move forward. It is never too late to reinvent yourself.

- I LEARNED – what self-love is and how to embody it. I learned how to transform my mindset, shatter my limiting beliefs and rewire my brain. I accomplished this through practicing daily affirmations, mirror work, meditation, yoga, prayer, read various personal development books, followed positive life coaches and people on Facebook, and filled my newsfeed with positivity. I also made a conscious effort to eat healthier and drink a minimum of eight, 8-ounce glasses of water a day to keep my body hydrated. We sometimes fail to realize that our thoughts shape our reality. Consistently feeding my mind positive self-talk and thoughts completely shifted my mindset.

- I RECOGNIZED – my weaknesses and created boundaries. Being an empath often makes it difficult to say no to people as if they are your responsibility. You want to help and heal everyone and tend to put their needs before your own. Empaths are highly-sensitive with keen abilities to sense what people around them are thinking and feeling. I learned to set healthy boundaries and limits for myself while unapologetically saying no to tasks that did not align with me.

- I JOURNALED – my thoughts and feelings daily. Anger, sadness, and fear became my normal reactions to the injustice we experienced. Journaling helped me release my feelings, as they spilled out onto the paper. It was so important for me to express my feelings and emotions such as anger, sadness, fear, hurt, and guilt in a healthy manner.

- I SURRENDERED – and repented to God. I did not grow up in a religious household and was new to this realm of God, religion, and spirituality. I bought a Bible and read it. I have become a Child of God and I am a spiritual being. I now make time to reflect, pray and meditate daily. My family and I are members of a church and attend worship often.

The aftermath of my abusive, traumatic life made me realize how much inner strength I had and how important it is to heal all the non-visible wounds that affect me emotionally, mentally, and spiritually. Reflecting, it truly makes me grateful for my journey and how much I have grown and evolved. I chose to share my life's journey in hopes that readers will gain insight and know healing is possible. There is a path to heal and regain your sense of self. It requires discipline, a daily conscious commitment and consumes most of your energy.

The tears will flow, your heart will ache,
and the pain may seem unbearable.
Hold on to hope, pray and keep the faith.

Healing after trauma is incredibly painful hard work. Day-by-day it will become easier. You will realize you are healing, gaining strength, and transforming.

During my healing journey, I kept my balance by making a conscious effort to keep my thoughts positive and my vibes high. I realized I had become a new version of myself. I learned that what other people think or say about me does not define who I am. Things I once tolerated became intolerable. I set healthy boundaries. The more I broke my silence and spoke my truth— the more I understood the value of my voice.

My children and I have been through the depths of hell, recovering from the heartache and pain we endured. Not only was it my responsibility to heal myself, it was also my responsibility to assure my children were healing and healthy as well. Things were progressing until a very recent development took everything off course again.

On Jan. 20, 2021 I learned that my 18-year-old son would not graduate high school with his class and would have to attend classes in the fall. Shortly after this meeting, I participated in a telemedicine appointment with my son's neurologist to discuss his recent MRI test results. As soon as the neurologist began talking, I knew from the tone of her voice the news was not going to be good. I learned my son has multiple severe traumatic brain injury (TBI). A TBI is caused by a bump, blow or jolt to the head that disrupts the normal function of the brain. It can be mild (concussion) or severe with long lasting effects. TBI is a major cause of death and disability in the United States.

My son's injury is the result of the verbal and physical abuse my ex-husband inflicted on him during his formative years when I was not around. It is the reason for his cognitive, social and important developmental delays.

The condition did not show up on MRIs following a seizure he had when he was 9 and another when he was 15. Now doctors believe the fact that he wore braces during those tests skewed the results. It was thought he would outgrow the seizures until the correct diagnosis was made earlier this year.

Research shows that individuals who experience severe TBI are likely to have lasting effects from their injury including cognitive function (attention and memory); motor function (weakness, impaired coordination and balance); sensation issues (hearing, vision, impaired perception and touch); and behavior issues depression, anxiety, aggression, emotional and behavioral control and personality changes). Individuals could also experience a reduced lifespan.

If you are a parent who has been in a domestic violent relationship I want to raise your awareness. If the abuse is happening to you, it is definitely affecting your children. More than likely they are being abused when you are not present. Keep in mind, perpetrators are good at "hiding" their wrong doings and like to groom their prey or make them swear to secrecy. The perpetrator may threaten to hurt you if the child or children tell anyone. This is exactly what happened in my home. They already saw me being hurt and sometimes, hurt so badly I was hospitalized, so they didn't want to cause me more pain.

Please, take the time to talk to your children.
Educate them on the red flags and warning signs.

Provide them with an action plan if they are ever in an uneasy situation. Know that the few minutes this conversation may "feel" uncomfortable, may actually save a life. If you are uncertain, reach out to your local community for more information and education. When a child is abused, they stop loving themselves NOT their abuser. My ex-husband, my son's biological father, completely changed the trajectory of my son's life.

The abuse stopped the day he left, yet the psychological effects and permanent injuries will be with him and us all the days of our lives. It really sucks that people can abuse, use and throw away people and permanently injure another human being — and still walk freely among us. Despite this, we will all persevere and rise.

I have awakened and evolved from a victim to a thriver! I am a being of peace, love and light; I emit and receive positive vibes and energy. I am a warrior who manifested my soulmate and true love. I transformed my fear into freedom and pain into peace. I have learned that our path is not a straight line — it is a spiral. Domestic Violence and Child Abuse are a multigenerational process. It will keep repeating unless you do something to stop it and break the cycle.

I am breaking generational cycles in my family through my healing. We do not realize how much inner strength we have until there is no other option. Through my transformation, I have discovered my passion and purpose. I am here to guide others to live their best life. I am a living testimony that you can hit rock bottom and start your life over. If I can do it, you can do it. What is possible for one is possible for all. Together we are stronger.

Abuse does not discriminate; it is a worldwide epidemic and occurs in all communities and zip codes. Whether we realize it or not, it affects all of us. The stigma and shame associated with it tend to keep victims and survivors silent and in dangerous environments.

I will continue to share my journey to let others know they are not alone, there is help and you too can heal and transform your life.

You own everything that happened to you.
Tell your stories.
If people wanted you to write warmly about them,
they should have behaved better.

~ Anne Lamott

Caroline Markel Hammond from Missouri
Photographed by Kelly Powell

Safe In Harm's Way

There is a beautiful Hebrew word — Talmud. It translates "to teach" and it is the comprehensive written version of the Jewish oral laws. One component states, "save one life, save the world."

This is my passion. This is my mission. Use confidence, patience, and truth to tell my story of surviving abuse, and celebrate what came after the abuse. All I need is to impact one person, and the world can begin to change.

If I were to share every aspect of the abuse my perpetrator issued over eight years, it would take an entire weekend and a case of wine. We would have to ZOOM call the FBI, plus go through two full-sized, four-drawer file cabinets. Consequently, I am narrowing the story down to one aspect — the physical and sexual abuse which I endured.

Since we do not have a weekend and given current time and travel constraints, we only have this book. I'm outrageously glad you're reading it. Thank you. But, honestly, I would like to be sitting across from you holding your hand.

Our conversation would go a little something like this, "Hello, dear friend. How are you? Been too long, right?"

"Wait," you're saying, "We don't even know each other."

But we will.

After this chapter, I hope we are best friends. I hope you feel less alone in the world and realize you have a life-long friend in me.

Ready to start? Here we go. Please do me a favor and do not let go of my hand until I finish my story. I need your strength and I am ready to offer mine in return.

It is vital in this discussion to not really focus on the person who abused me. Therefore there will be shadowy outlines of him, but the focus will be on how I dealt with the abuse. Besides, it is not about him.

This is about me.

This is my life.

My healing.

My future.

My hope, in hearing my story and sharing my outcome, is that you can recognize yourself or someone you love. I never want another person to feel the deep shame, sadness and regret which comes with surviving abuse from a man who claimed to love me; and, at the same time, issued horrific and diseased abuse which could easily send me crying, running, and cowering in fear.

I want my story to fuel your knowledge and vocabulary, allowing you to rise from abuse so the journey becomes about you.

Your life.

Your healing.

Your future.

Let us set a baseline. Sure, the physical abuse encompassed the usual definition — throwing me against tables, spitting in my face, chasing me through the house screaming at me, grabbing the steering wheel and trying to run us off the road. The usual and so much more other people face, too. But let me be crystal clear here, the biggest components of his physical abuse stemmed from the hundreds of affairs he had with men and women, without my knowledge (and 100 percent without my consent) and then came back home and had unprotected sex with me; exposing me to the possibility of all manner of sexually transmitted diseases.

I thought we were in a committed and monogamous relationship. Why would I ever make him use a condom? Turns out, that was the furthest thing from the truth.

As the 1987 George Michael song "I want your sex," plays, imagine it as background music while we talk about the rise of online avenues to secure sex across the world. During our talk, we focus on two of the many sites I discovered permeated every day of my relationship with the man I almost married, and I had zero idea how much I was put in harm's way.

Adult Friend Finders. This "sex positive" website had an estimate of 412 million accounts. You did not read that wrong — 412 million. Million. Its data was breached in November of 2016, just days after I was informed of my abuser's long-term participation with his main male sex partner in this online forum.

The next player in this elaborate charade is Craigslist. The "Casual Encounters" section allowed users to seek sex with strangers while they also looked for used cars and furniture.

It's hard to get an accurate number of users because Craigslist didn't track this section and it was closed down in 2018 due to the amount of human sex trafficking taking place and the proliferation of child rape videos. This was my perpetrator's favorite spot. The filth I discovered and given to me by anonymous sources caused me to begin vomiting.

At the time of these data breaches, I was living my own personal hell of discovery. This was either a beautiful wink from the universe in the synchronicities of my life unraveling, or the laughter of gods I still cannot decide which. I do know this — just as Medusa was banished in Greek god lore, I went from living in a 4,900 square foot house to being homeless, and finally a tiny 1,042 square-foot apartment tucked in a huge complex in the hopes of staying hidden.

Let me pause here. This is dry information, right? Can I get you another blanket? Do you need a restroom break, because now would be a good time before we get into the nitty-gritty.

On the low end, we have 412 million people choosing to cheat on their spouse. I mean maybe there are cross-over users on all platforms with multiple accounts, but this is still a high number. Do you know what did not happen? No one talked about the consequences for the partners of those 412 million users. The partners, like me, who had zero idea the person they believed was monogamous was arranging sex online with strangers. Imagine!

Imagine if I got only 5 percent of the partners to step forward.
It would be almost 21 million people with ideas
and information to change the world.
Those 21 million people would not feel alone in shame.

Let's start to connect the dots, please. Let us imagine the *Adult Friend Finders* user is the vice president or director of a publicly traded company. This person uses his company cell phone to text and arrange for sex with people he has never met. I never knew, but I discovered it is easy. Really. Easy. When the person travels, the zip code is changed and any available person in the new city is pulled up for sex, too. He is using company collateral to personally advertise with strangers and posting his picture on the CL website. This allows for any person who agrees to meet him easy access with his corporate cell phone number and personal picture.

Here is the first dot to connect — a quick reverse number look-up on Google and the phone is traced back to his company in less than 41 seconds. Plus, his picture? Well having the company information, any person (or jealous partner) can use LinkedIn to trace his picture, with the newly found company, and BOOM! You know exactly who you are meeting up with for sex.

Can these strangers show up to his place of business? Yes, they could. If anyone is intent on causing harm, are other employees at risk? Yes. Statistics show that when violence is aimed at an individual in the workplace, an additional 20 percent of employees have the risk of being a casualty. Consequently, the online user is risking his employer and fellow employees. Yet, no one talked about this line of ugly potential in the data breach.

Here I am, believing in our monogamy, and he is choosing to have sex with any man or woman with an orifice. This type of exposure to STDs is another reality that no one talked about in all the data breaches. The very real fact is that a survivor must summon enough courage, fight through shame and show up to the doctor's office for sexually transmitted disease testing. Oh!!! And the wait. The wait for results is enough to find you crying on the bathroom floor of a public restroom, unable to get up and really not caring about the last time the floor was mopped. No wait; that was me.

Discovering these happy-ass sexcapades was a layer of filth I could not soak off my skin. Honey, I took a lot of baths. Three hours long, filling and re-filling the tub. Scaring my kids who would knock on the door, "Please. Mom. Please get out of the tub." Sad. Scared. Absolutely fucking furious.

> *My anger at his actions were the obvious ones*
> *of betrayal and lies. But the potential to compromise*
> *my future sexuality was a factor, too.*

I love sex. I love everything about it. The discovery. The smell, taste, tangles and invested exploration of another soul is the most fun thing I think a human can do. I chose wisely over the course of my life. I chose sparingly. Now I was facing the potential of my sex life being altered forever because of him.

Man oh man! The healing needed for this dotted-line-connection was huge. Again, therapy. Always therapy.

I went to therapy immediately! Domestic violence shelters have free therapy groups and you don't have to live there to attend sessions. Your work employee assistance plan may have three to five sessions for free with a counselor. It will take more sessions, but most therapists can use a sliding scale, based on your income, to negotiate a payment. I started talking. I chose to cast shame aside and asked for help.

Do you recognize yourself in any of this? Here is the moment I can offer tools and ideas, pull you up off the bathroom floor. Now you know you are not the only person who has ever experienced this type of abuse. Plus, know there are invested folks in this component of healing who want to help. Ask. Finally, remember you have me. I am one person, and one person can change the world.

I had multiple tests. I visited multiple doctors. I talked to the top infectious disease specialist in the area and the knowledge I gained is beautiful. The worry fell from me, allowing healing to progress at a comfortable pace. The sexual relationships I have entered into "after" have been the most fun, armed with all my knowledge and healing work. The fear that my past abuse would scare away relationships was not true. Men often thought it was a completely anarchist move to choose to heal and fight the good fight for other women. The encouragement I received fuels my soul and the men remain, even if the romance did not take. I have also found the opposite experience and this is where the down-to-my-soul belief in the best people staying in your world, and the wrong people leaving, bring moments of gratitude.

I hope my personal experience helps you and anyone else who has had the experience of numerous affairs from their abuser. Knowledge is power, baby. It is scary as hell, my dear. Key takeaway? Do not feel shame. You are not alone. There is help. Please check out page 141-142 for additional resources.

***I would sound like a complete and total jerk
if I didn't point out there are friends I have made
on this journey of healing, who have suffered huge
physical consequences from the sexual choices of their abuser.***

Every time I hear a truth spoken in this arena, I am an instant mix of sadness, compassion, and fury. We have additional resources available within this realm. The healing is longer, but the truth of not being alone on the journey is there, too. Plus, there are fabulous future sexual relationships in this version of "after" too. Talking about our journeys together helps further dispel shame. If we all hold hands and speak our truth, then no one needs to feel alone.

The picture we are creating is starting to emerge as more dots are connected. How the psychological implications play out with physical and sexual abuse for me would take longer to untangle because the disease he issued seeped into many arenas. Craigs list? UGH!! Don't even get me started on Craigslist. Google the many stories on Craigslist and you will find people being killed over household purchases and women being raped due to their information and locations being posted by angry ex-husbands. Men who encouraged CL members to find their former partner and rape her; and people showed up to do it!

> *The more I searched and learned about Craigslist,*
> *the more disgusted I became. There were groups*
> *the abuser visited which discussed how to drug*
> *your girlfriend and watch while other men raped her.*

This explained why many of his emails to the forum began with, "My girlfriend has no idea I am doing this to her, but she will be at this place at this time" and then giving out my picture, where I would be and what I did for a living. Year after year, picture after picture, I discovered he had been offering me up for sex with other people, without my knowledge and without my consent. Each post included the words, "My girlfriend has no idea I am doing this." Or, "My girlfriend is hot. You should see what she looks like." And the ever present in almost every email, "I will facilitate what we discussed could be done to her."

Yeah, I would not find out about all the unknown activity, until I was informed of all this secret information on his computer.

What was he going to have done to me? Drug me? Allow these Craigslist contacts to rape me? Book me out for future dates to drug and rape me? He sent this out to multiple people!!! How the heck was he going to pull this all off? I have no idea.

I do know this. I am haunted by the what-ifs to this day. There are nights I do not remember; which I only discovered occurred via his secret email account. Plus, our normal nightly routine was to have sex and he would bring me a glass of wine after. Is that when it happened? Did he drug me in the wine offering and allow people to sneak into the house to rape me? Our master bedroom door connected directly to the deck on the back of the house. How many times did we have date nights where the sole reason was not his love for me, but an opportunity for his Craigslist contacts to check me out and reserve "facilitating what could be done to me." Me? Well in this scenario, I am the chick who woke up knowing I had sex with him the night before; so there would be nothing physically different about me or within me. I would have zero clue. Clearly this is sex trafficking. This is offering someone up for sex without their consent.

How many strangers have my pictures now?
How many strangers know me intimately?

Craigslist was his favorite source to seek out sexual partners. He used it consistently for a total of 18 years — eight years with me for the entirety of our relationship. How many people did he try to pimp me out to? I'm hoping someday to find out. All I need is one person to step forward, right? No one talks about this in a data breach. No one talks about all the implications of this type of physical and sexual abuse. The tentacles are ugly when the mechanism used is ugly.

I am taking all these unknowns in my life and channeling them into my company called Epizon Strategy Solutions. My business works with organizations to bring awareness of how abusers operate and the associated risks to a corporation's reputation, profitability and the lives of its employees. Drawing on Human Resources and Business degrees, plus 30 years of training and development experience, we create corporate training to expose abuse, implement policy with year-round touchpoints and hold perpetrators accountable. There are about 469 million reasons for corporations to protect their profitability, reputation, and biggest investment in the people they employ. Can you imagine the consequences of abusers being terminated for ignoring corporate policy? I may not ever know what happened to me, but I can ensure I am doing my part to stop the fastest growing industry in the United States — human sex trafficking.

Here are some additional dots needing to be connected — the entire family is affected. Inherent in the choice to fuck strangers in the abuser's own home, he exposes everyone in his family to danger.

This is a perfect example of people not taking the next steps of what exactly those kinds of actions could mean to everyone who lives in the same house with an adulterer who uses the internet to secure his next partner. These strangers could have come back. They could have harmed my kids. They could have harmed his kids. Hell, if they really wanted to cause harm, they had pictures to know what each child liked and tuition bills in the kitchen mail pile to look through for contact.

Strangers knew where we lived. Strangers saw pictures of our family. Strangers saw the beautifully framed family photos from our local magazine cover story about being the perfect blended family. Ha!

I had to sit my kids down and talk to them about being aware of not only the abuser as a threat, but also to have heightened awareness around anyone they thought seemed "weird." I didn't know who could show up looking for us.

I hatched a plan, friend.

I did not sleep as I tried to find every single person I could. And it was outrageously easy to find the people he connected with for sex.

I easily found the names and addresses of people, plus their friends and family. It got to be a game. I would time myself from start to finish. My average got to be less than five minutes for the person and five family/friend connections. I could be unstoppable in less than seven minutes for the person and ten family/friend connections.

Pretty cool, huh? But guess what? This means those people could also find me just as easily. And they did. This took the form of anonymous people on Facebook and Craigslist who tracked me down via messenger to email to let me know of his actions. How did they find me? Well they knew my name from being in my home, they knew what I looked like from pictures and a quick Google search found all tax records with my name. People (there were many different sources) had been so disgusted with the sexual encounters they had with him, or maybe what he was trying to plan for me, they decided to expose him to me.

Plus, I have a sneaking suspicion someone at his place of employment was a source of information, too. It would be like magic. I'd receive all the search history of his computer and his Facebook searches for people. It became a way to double check and know the people matched up from all the sources I received. Once he connected with people on CL, he also searched them and their family on Facebook. Consistently, I mean like weekly, for years! It was beautiful and filthy at the same time. Pissed off, yet full of gratitude. Scared.

Where is the healing here, and how can fear be fought? I learned huge lessons on speaking out. You might want to highlight these next couple paragraphs, tab them with a post-it note and read them often, please.

No one listens to the crying, screaming woman wronged.

No one. Not that people don't care, because they do. However, it's scary. The abuse you speak of is scary to others, and coupled with scream-cry, makes folks back away.

Being calm is hard. I wasn't calm for many moons. I was a crying, cursing, screaming lunatic when I talked to people. I couldn't gain control. I was scared and sad and it showed in every word which came spilling out of my mouth and the snot which ran down my nose. Or, the 12-page-long text rants I'd send to people. People backed away from me. Why would they not?

Here is what finally worked for me. Using therapy to speak my truth in a calm way. Of course, there can be tears. I'm not saying I was robotic. But if I started each conversation with the simple sentence, "I am really scared and confused and I am hoping you can help me," eventually I got to a space where I could proceed with few tears.

Beautiful outcome — people did not run and they helped me or sent me to someone who could. I talked about abuse to my new neighbors, friends, family, police, lawyers, judges, and the FBI. My honesty brought referrals and eventually I'd find the right person to help; like my FBI contact. Our connection, after discovering the significance of his secret life and associations, is maintaining his high frequency on their radar. Plus, so is anyone who is associated with his abuse or keeps his company now.

After about four months of living in my new neighborhood, I baked batch upon batch of brownies. I went and introduced myself to my six closest neighbors. They got copies of my restraining orders, with his name blacked out. I asked them for help — from calling the cops when screaming is heard to awareness around people looking or asking for me. Consequently, my neighbors check on me constantly, and the awareness created has allowed us to be close as neighbors and humans.

None of this would have happened,
had I lived in silent shame.

I hope everyone is seeing a pattern here! Talking about it changes one person, or six neighbors, and lives get better because I calmly asked for help.

Also, BIG NEWS! A survivor can hide all public information (like those pesky tax records!) through US State programs which hide the address of victims of violence. Every state has a system and the information is page 141-142. I used it and signed up kids, too.

All these dots connected for discovery and healing created a picture of "too much" for a few years. Too much vomit, welts, crying in bed, crying on the floor, crying in my car and baths. Wondering when I last brushed my teeth. Fear. Sadness. Anger. Unable to sleep. Sleeping for 16 hours. Too much booze. Too many pills. Too much Jalapeno Krunchers potato chips. "Too much" is all the tiny moments in the lines drawn connecting one dot to the next.

But wait — there's more. Please do not stop holding my hand.

Please do not walk away and close this book. We must get to the show-closing healing reveal. It's there. Promise.

Strike up the marching band and cue the fireworks; I now know none of this was my fault.

None of your abuse is your fault.

You (me, us) trusted and believed the person who looked us in the eyes and claimed undying and monogamous love, but then met random people for sex in parking garages or behind the local community college up the street. The reality of exposing you without knowledge or consent is there, too.

In your own home.

In your own bed.

You did not deserve this treatment. You are worthy of so much more and better.

I know perfectly what this "too much" shame feels like. It is a heavy coat smelling of three-day old cigarette smoke, cat pee and dirty lake water. Yes, that coat of shame hanging on the coat rack in the corner.

Guess what? It starts to shrink when it is put into bright sunlight.

My own version of sunlight is this non-profit foundation called **Safe in Harm's Way**. I created it for both survivors and those who love them. **Safe In Harm's Way's** goal is to connect survivors and all their "too much" dots. We offer a community and every resource a survivor needs to heal.

As I built **Safe In Harm's Way**, I became very bold about my story online using Facebook and LinkedIn to detail abuse options and strategy for healing. The more I spoke, the more magic came into my world. My dear friend Kristi once told me, "The entirety of the abuse you endured is massive and horrific, I'm not sure anyone can comprehend fully what you lived through. And the beauty, magic, love, world-wide travel and connections you have made in your 'after' are also amazing. It's unreal." (She is right. I'm documenting it all for the next book!) I also have dreams of creating an affordable conference where survivors can gather and celebrate their bad-ass selves. There will be dancing, there will be celebrating. There will be discussion groups with ideas shared and next steps to implement as we march back to our lives and change the damn world. It's really gonna be a thing. Matching t-shirts and crowns even. Promise.

In addition, I had the beauty of others reaching out to me. I've never spoken his name. I never will. However, people I knew and loved for years began reaching out to me once my return to social media also included a relationship vacancy. I heard from people I cut off because I no longer knew who I could trust. Folks randomly started popping up in unexpected ways; some interactions were simply encouraging me in my non-profit work and entrepreneurial start-up. Many others disclosed their true view of the man I escaped, with the same courtesy of never speaking his name to me.

The sentiments were the same whether personal or professioal; he had never been liked or respected from about the second grade forward to his professional industry. It was me who raised his reputation from the gutter, and when I escaped, back to the gutter he fell. Fast. My choice to speak about my advocacy for survivors of abuse, even while never uttering his name, fueled and fixed connections spanning decades.

Life after abuse can be incredibly hard, but I tell you ...... the stinky coat of shame, sadness and embarrassment shrinks to 10 sizes too small when you use confidence, patience, and truth to share your story. Oh!! Always remember to be calm. You will be surprised by the number of people who confide their own coat size to you, too. You are never alone.

We need just one person (or, you know, 21 million) to step forward into the light. Join me. Take my hand and let's go change the world.

List of Resources from Caroline Markel Hammond:

1. How to easily reach Caroline Markel Hammond and receive free offers for healing, help, guidance and meditation: https://carolinemarkelhammond.replynow.ontraport.net/

2. Listing by State for the Safe at Home Personal Information Removal Program: https://www.sos.mo.gov/business/SafeAtHome/Address ConfidentialityProgramsByState

3. Best Blog for Diagnosis and Navigating Exposures to STD: https://www.stdcheck.com/blog

4. Best Blog for How to Reclaim Your LIfe after a STD diagnosis: https://thestiproject.com/

5. Real life and focused on zero shame. This blog is amazing and I promise it will help you heal. The author has categorized all the posts. While she is not actively engaging now, you will find a wealth of information and stop the cycle of shame. Really. You're not alone! https://earthwindandherpes.tumblr.com/

6. Did you know you do NOT have to live in a domestic violence shelter to take advantage of their services? It's true. Use this simple zip code tool and find the shelter closest to you and attend their free services from counseling to lawyer advocacy to completing any required paperwork as you navigate leaving your abuser. https://www.domesticshelters.org/

7. Want to know how you can properly collect evidence against your abuser? BOOM! Here you go. Check out these fabulous people at Victims Voice app: https://victimsvoice.app/

8. Need a community of group therapy done on ZOOM with people from around the world? Want a special focus on narcissistic abuse and codependency? Here you go. These coaches and therapy options are amazing and can be done from a variety of time and day options, with real-life people who have lived and survived what you are now experincing.
   https://www.thelivingwellcoaching.com/

9. Of course, there is my personal favorite site where you can find the vocabulary needed to properly label what is happening in your life, so that you can create a future free from abuse.
   https://safeinharmsway.org/

Your abuser is only as strong as your silence.

~ Najwa Zebian

About the Authors

Alisa Divine, Michigan

Alisa coaches women to write their stories, build platforms as leaders and create impact through books and businesses. She is the CEO of Personal Power Press, author of Next Generation Indie Book Award Finalist, *#SheWins*, and co-author of Amazon bestsellers, *Killing Kate* and *She Rises*. Alisa is the host of *#SheWins* Podcast.

In addition, Alisa founded The More Than Beautiful Project™. Through this online course she mentors women to build confidence, develop a positive mindset and choose healthy relationships. She has been a featured guest expert at global summits, conferences, TV shows, in print media and on SiriusXM, iHeart Media, Entercom and Florida Public Radio. Her appearances include several big cities from Boston and Detroit to Minneapolis and San Diego.

Alisa is on the Board of Directors of the Saginaw Underground Railroad, which serves survivors of domestic violence. She lives in Michigan with her husband and blended family.

Visit *www.alisadivine.com* to get info on her weekend retreats, coaching, courses, or to seek help writing your own book or short story.

https://www.facebook.com/alisa.divine

Staci Austin, Texas

Staci was raised in the small town of Farmington, NM until she turned 15 years old. Then she moved 15 miles outside of Hutchinson, KS to an all girls Christian Boarding School where she graduated high school. Staci currently resides in the Austin, TX area.

She spent many years directing and owning a Childcare Center and is a recent foster parent. Staci has been a Real Estate Agent in the Austin, TX area since 2006.

Staci is committed to helping the homeless and disabled. She also volunteers at an orphanage and her dream as a child was to own one. She will be continuing her mission work in Kenya, Africa and plans to travel to many other countries to learn their cultures. She loves ballet, playing the piano, music, snow skiing and going to the beach.

Staci would like to provide support to women who need help getting out of abusive situations. She is currently writing a book about abuse.

staci.shewins2@gmail.com

https://www.facebook.com/stacidyannaustin

Courtney Petersen, Texas

Courtney is the Founder and CEO of **SPEAK Cosmetics**. She launched her business from her personal experience of domestic abuse. She saw the need to make resources available and build a community of hope. Through stories that women relate to and share, she said they will know they are not alone.

Her 17 years of experience in the cosmetics business as a national artist and trainer, motivates her passion for color. She sees how women can be transformed by the power of makeup. SPEAK Cosmetics exists for a cause — every color a story, every story from a survivor, every survivor sharing hope.

Courtney is also passionate about training individuals in personal and professional growth. She works full time as an Area Vice President for Sales and Training with CareCredit. She lives in Austin, TX along with her husband Ben, her two toddler sons Logan and Leo and her stepson, Lukas. She loves exploring her own city with family and friends, running, hiking, food sampling and entertaining. What fuels Courtney most is her faith.

You can shop and share stories on her website:
www.speakcosmetics.com

https://www.facebook.com/speakcosmetics

https://www.instagram.com/speakcosmetics

Renee Courier Aumock, Michigan

Renee recognizes injustice and searches for opportunities to lead positive change. She is a motivational speaker who encourages people, especially women and girls, to rise above challenges and create the positive life they deserve. Renee currently serves on the Good Samaritan Rescue Mission Board. She is a motivational speaker for the YWCA Getting Ahead Program, and is the founder of **From Pain to Purpose** Facebook page.

Renee has worked in post-secondary planning for more than 15 years and experienced a positive transformation in her own life after completing her higher education. Being a first-generation college graduate, she clearly understands the importance of career planning assistance. Her goal is to ensure that everyone knows they can gain training and employment in any field they enjoy and are gifted to work. As a non-traditional student, full-time employee and single mom, Renee obtained her bachelor's degree in Business with a minor in Health Information Management and a master's in Strategic Management.

Please connect with her on her Facebook Page: **From Pain to Purpose** or at *Reneecourier@gmail.com*

Brandi Smith, Arkansas

Brandi is a 48-year-old single mom of two beautiful children, a 25-year old daughter and a 15-year old son. She spent 16 wonderful years working in the medical field. She is an advocate against domestic violence and sexual assault.

Her near-death experience at the hands of her abusive husband occurred at her daughter's 21st birthday party. Brandi's story received national attention following TV news coverage in Arkansas and Tennessee. As a result, she appeared twice on the daytime television show, *The Doctors*, telling her story and even receiving major eye surgery on camera to help repair her vision. She has spoken at local and regional events, churches and colleges sharing her experiences and encouraging victims to speak up and speak out. She has been featured in *Take a Break*, a magazine in the United Kingdom.

Brandi volunteers at the Women's Shelter of Central Arkansas. One day, she intends to start her own nonprofit helping women as well as men overcome life after domestic violence or sexual violence.

Connect with her on *Facebook @Brandi Smith.*

Christina Williams, Pennsylvania

Christina is a survivor and advocate against domestic violence. She specialized in prevention education at her local women's shelter where she was once a client. That was the the steppingstone to her advocacy work and social media platforms.

After she left her abuser, she realized that there were only a few online resources that addressed domestic violence and healing. So she took action. She is the founder and creator of the Facebook page **Damsels-N-Distress**. Her goal is to provide accessible information for victims/survivors of domestic violence and sexual assault. The site aims to help trauma victims identify narcissistic abusive behavior and understand what abusers do and how. The resources promote healing and hope. There also are empowering quotes to build self-esteem. Currently, the site has more than 13,000 followers. Christina also has a large advocacy platform on LinkedIn@Christina Williams.

Christina recently graduated from Lock Haven University with a degree in Criminal Justice. She plans to help victims/survivors in the courtroom setting. She resides in Pennsylvania with her 11-year-old son. Please feel free to email Christina, ***christinakunes@yahoo.com.***

Rodelyn Daguplo, Melbourne, Australia

Rodelyn was born in the Philippines but left her homeland to begin a relationship in Australia. After 11 years of physical and psychological abuse, she finally moved out. To build her self confidence after the trauma, she began successfully competing in beauty pageants.

She is the current President of The Women Association Inc. and the cover queen of the World Class Beauty Queens Magazine Issue 123, January 2021. She is also a candidate for World Class Woman of the Year 2021. In addition, she holds the following beauty queen and charity titles: International Asian Mum of the Year 2019 Ambassador; Mrs. Timeless Beauty Ambassador of Earth 2019; Mrs. International Asian Mum of the Year Mindanao Philippines; and 2nd runner up Philippine Fiesta of Victoria Queen and Charity 2018.

Rodelyn is the owner of Queen Lyn Travel and Tours, Queen Lyn Health and Beauty, and Queen Lyn Gown Rentals. She is currently employed as a part-time nurse assistant and a part-time disability support practitioner.

She is the proud mother of two beautiful children — Alexander, 7 and Christy, 5. Rodelyn empowers and advocates for women and children affected by domestic violence and the elderly with disabilities.

Connect with her on *Facebook: Rodelyn Daguplo*

email: rodelyndaguploshewins2@gmail.com

Brandy Reese Sloan, Texas

Brandy's goal has always been to make a positive impact on the world with music. When her abuser nearly killed her including breaking both of her arms and crushing her fingers, she was determined to heal.

Today, Brandy is remarried to a wonderful man and together they own and operate a small music school, Sinfonia Music Academy, where she is able to share her love of music every day. She continues to be an advocate for survivors of domestic violence raising awareness by marching in rallies, speaking on panels and educating teenage girls about healthy relationships. She also uses her musical gifts to give back to the community. She spearheaded the implementation of a children's music program at the Battered Women's and Children's Shelter in San Antonio.

Brandy also volunteers her time with the LGSM Foundation, an organization that assists individuals with special needs in private music study. She is also a foster parent. In addition to playing and teaching music, Brandy enjoys cooking, crafting and playing with her three dogs, Baldwin, Zoë, and Willie.

brandyshewinstoo@gmail.com

HelenMarie McCracken, Arizona

HelenMarie is a Master Practitioner of Neuro-Linguistic Programming (NLP), Success Life Coach, Hypnotherapist, Practitioner of Time Integration for Maximum Empowerment (T.I.M.E.) Techniques, Practitioner of Emotional Freedom Techniques (EFT) and a registered member of the International Board of Coaches and Practitioners (IBCP). She is also a nationally certified victim's domestic and sexual violence advocate. All of that aside, her greatest accomplishment is being a wife and mother.

She never dreamed of finding herself in a relationship consumed by domestic violence — until the day she did. Prior to that, she wasn't even sure what domestic violence was or how to identify it. From that day forward, she decided to dedicate her life to "breaking the silence" of domestic violence, child abuse, and personality disorders by educating communities with the ultimate goal of breaking the stigma.

HelenMarie, through adversity and perseverance, has taken what she learned and created **HM3 Advocate, Inc.**, a 501c3 organization servicing southern Arizona. The organization prides itself in offering holistic tools and resources to empower survivors of abuse. The key — educate and advocate the way there.

Facebook:
https://www.facebook.com/hm3advocate

https://www.facebook.com/hm3traumarecoveryspecialist

Instagram:

@hm3traumacoach

@hm3advocate

https://www.hm3.me

Caroline Markel Hammond, Missouri

The 2020 Boston Scientific Global Volunteer and the Vera Bradley Inspiring Women Award winner, Caroline has spent 30 years as a results-driven sales and training professional promoting billion-dollar brands for Fortune 500 companies. Her successful career excels in sales, human resources, training and development.

In addition, she is the CEO and founder of **Safe In Harm's Way**. On its website and social media platforms, people can find resources to help identify their abuse, escape their situation and heal from their trauma.Caroline leads a team of 15 incredible volunteers who take hands to change the world for survivors of abuse. Safe In Harm's Way's founding pillar is inclusive of the unique perspective needed by people of color, men, LGBTQ community and abuse survivors.

As a survivor of domestic violence, Caroline uses storytelling to evoke change. She has been featured in *Forbes, PBS, NPR* and partnerships with Out of Home Advertising Association of America (OAAA), national and regional television, and podcasts. She is a thought leader in the domestic violence and overcoming adversity arenas, plus international training implementation and curriculum.

www.safeinharmsway.org

*Strength doesn't come from what you can do.
It comes from overcoming the things
you once thought you couldn't.*

~ Rikki Rogers

About the Photographers

Trish Hadley is a full-time photographer with a studio in Old Town Saginaw. She started a portrait + boudoir business in 2014 after being a graphic designer for 15 years and photographing mostly Detroit + Traverse area weddings with her husband, Patrick. Now she specializes in photographing women of all ages/shapes and the best part of her job is making everyday women feel gorgeous during and after their shoot (when they view images).

Her client base is from all over Michigan and she is grateful to be able to work with so many awesome women from around the state!

Trish Hadley, Michigan
https://trishhadleyboudoir.com/
https://www.instagram.com/trish.hadley.boudoir/

Michelle Loconto was born and raised in Dallas, Texas. Michelle has been documenting authentic and sentimental moments through her lens for 20+ years. She brings a sophisticated perspective to the art of photography, and is focused on making every client feel confident and relaxed in front of the camera. Working alongside industry leaders and world-renowned photographers, she now fuses her expertise with her own creative vision to operate her studio, LocoLens. Her patience, creativity and unwavering attention to detail are what guide her in capturing emotionally-moving images that tell a unique story.

Michelle Loconto, Texas
Featured in: *NSIDE Magazine, D Magazine, Brides magazine,*
Spectacular Weddings of Texas, Tribeza magazine, Fortune magazine
Bride's Choice Award – *2018, 2017, 2016, 2015, 2014, 2013, 2012,*
2011, 2010, 2009

LocoLens.com   hello@locolens.com   512-669-8885

Jenni Roberts is a photographer in Taylor, Texas. She started her business, Jenni Roberts Photography, in 2010 and never looked back. With every photo shoot, whether professional, family or otherwise, her desire is to help people see the beauty in their own lives. She believes one beautiful photo can show a person that moments they thought were ordinary - selling products, snuggling kids - may just be the moments they are living out their dreams. Jenni earned a history degree from Baylor University. She lives in Taylor with her husband Michael, her son Sam, and daughter Annie. Free time finds her reading, road tripping around Texas with her kids and volunteering at her local church.

Jenni Roberts, Texas
https://www.jennirobertsphotography.com/

Monica Westbrook is a portrait photographer in Benton, Arkansas. Her love for photography started 17 years ago when her son, Gunnar, was born. What started as a hobby has turned into a successful business. Her daughter Rhyan was born six years ago, and that sparked a new interest — newborn photography to the mix. She is a self-taught photographer that enjoys learning all the newest trends and techniques.

Monica also holds a degree in cardio-respiratory care and works as a respiratory therapist at a local hospital. Some of her other hobbies include singing, watching and playing basketball, antiquing with friends, traveling, and spending time with family.

Monica Westbrook, Arkansas
facebook.com/monicawestbrookphotography
IG @MonicaWestbrookPhotography
clickchick81@gmail.com
501-317-8996

Hannah Trott - Dear Grace Photography is a sister photography team based out of Lock Haven, Pennsylvania. Brittany and Hannah mainly focus on weddings and families, but also strive to empower people through their boudoir work and portrait sessions. Some words from the sisters: "It's love that weaves together the tapestry of our lives and composes the songs of our souls. It joins families, communities, and cultures. Love is why we're here; on this planet and in this business." This focus on love being the reason for everything helps the photography duo see the world in a unique way and helps clients see it that way as well. Dear Grace was honored to work on this special project set with the vision of empowering people to rise up as a phoenix does from the ashes.

Hannah Trott, Pennsylvania
Dear Grace Photography
Brittany Martin & Hannah Trott
Lock Haven, Pennsylvania
www.deargracephotography.com
instagram: @deargracephotos
fb: Dear Grace Photography
Brittanymartin@deargracephotography.com
570-367-1589

Angelito Valdez Jr. is a freelance photographer based in Melbourne, Australia. His journey into photography began as a way to record his own children. He then took the plunge, pursuing a growing interest in photographing nature, particularly landscapes, seascapes, flowers and birds. A friend strongly encouraged him to consider wedding photography. During that time, he learned a vast array of techniques and skills. He decided to turn his passion into a part-time business.

Currently his photography work encompasses weddings, birthdays, pre-nuptial and modeling shoots, as well as many other styles. His works have been featured in different magazines including *MOB*, *Moevir, Edith* and *INTRA*.

He describes his photography as honest, sincere and intimate. His primary focus now is the beauty and raw emotions found in each moment he captures. He loves the romance in weddings and the delight and innocence of children and others who model in his photography.

Angelito Valdez Jr, Melbourne, Australia
https://www.facebook.com/angelitovaldezjr.photography/

Jessica Korff is the owner and creative mind behind Fleur de Lea Photography and *REfashiond Magazine*. Her mission is to be an impactful force for good for women business owners, helping them to find their confidence and power, and the self-permission to step into that. She believes when women finally stop playing small, and start showing up unapologetically the world will change.

While much of her focus is on headshots and branding, her work with helping women find their strength and self-love does not end there. In January of 2020 she launched a local women in business magazine where the primary goal is to support women in growth, collaborations and inspiration, encouraging the "marriage" of power and femininity. The name REfashiond comes because as women, we just do success differently. In January of 2021 she kicked off another way to lift women in their strength and power, through a project called The Art of Her, where she creates portraits and tells the stories of local women who, despite the things meant to keep them small, still rise.

Jessica Korff, Arizona   www.FDLphoto.com   jessica@FDLphoto.com
@FleurdeLea_JessicaKorff   520.975.9051

163

Kelly Powell is an artist and Kansas City native. While in college she discovered photography. It was a way to bridge the gap of her love for art and her passion for people. After graduating and taking a full-time position at a studio, she got an opportunity of a lifetime working on a documentary crew. They documented the recovery efforts in Sierra Leone after the blood diamond wars ended. That experience catapulted her into a life of entrepreneurship and mentorship. Kelly opened her own photography and design studio in 2008 shortly after returning home where giving back to the community and outreach through art and photography has become common place within her business model. Kelly lives in Kansas City with her husband and their 3 year old son that keeps them moving and shaking. When she isn't working she loves hanging out with friends and family, traveling, being outdoors, making good food, listening to music and watching all of the movies.

Kelly Powell, Missouri   Elements Studio Photography
1324 W. 12th St (West Bottoms)   816.739.3491
Kansas City, MO 64111
elementsphotostudio@gmail.com
www.elementsphotostudio.com